THE OFFICIAL® PRICE GUIDE TO

Sewing Collectibles

❀❀❀❀❀❀❀❀❀❀

JOYCE CLEMENT

FIRST EDITION

THE HOUSE OF COLLECTIBLES
NEW YORK, NEW YORK 10022

Cover photo © Tender Buttons

Published by: The House of Collectibles
201 East 50th Street
New York, New York 10022

Distributed by Ballantine Books, a division of Random House, Inc., New York and simultaneously in Canada by Random House of Canada Limited, Toronto.

Manufactured in the United States of America

ISBN: 0-876-37747-9

10 9 8 7 6 5 4 3 2

Table of Contents

🪶🪶🪶🪶🪶🪶🪶🪶🪶🪶🪶

Acknowledgments

❀❀❀❀❀❀❀❀❀❀❀❀

I give special thanks and gratitude to my children, Amy and Ross, for their patience and help during the preparation of this book. They not only gave their help, but more importantly their moral support. Without that I do not believe it could have been done.

I have had extremely competent statistical and clerical help from Amy Clement and Carolyn Arner, and this has certainly made my job easier.

A very special thanks is in order to Darla Molnar for the photographic work that she so generously and competently provided.

Introduction

❀❀❀❀❀❀❀❀❀❀

The implements or tools used during sewing and needlework have always been very important in the antique and collectibles market. Items such as thimbles, buttons, sewing tables and stands, spinning wheels, yarn winders and early irons have long been desired by collectors. Now, recent trends are seeing the whole realm of related sewing and needlework items commanding a market of their own.

One of the most appealing things about collecting anything related to sewing and needlework, is that a novice collector can easily begin by simply looking around their own home. History has proven that every homemaker is involved with some form of sewing, mending or embroidery. Every home has a sewing box or basket, and there is an absolute delight in searching through these to find all that has accumulated over the years. With its share of buttons, pins and pincushions, needles, and even old magazines, you have the start of a collection before you know it. Many sewing tools have changed in form slightly or not at all over the ages, so they will be relatively easy to recognize. Once you have gathered all your collectibles study them closely, for a long and fascinating history is involved with each and every item.

The history of sewing and needlework spans the history of humankind. From the time that people donned clothing they have had to put them together in some fashion, hence, the art of sewing began. People have always felt the need to express their individuality, they never merely covered themselves, but rather adorned themselves and their possessions. The adornment of clothing in some manner or form has always been a reflection of the culture in which the seamstress lived. To gain insight into the values and customs of a particular culture or era, one need only take a careful look at the decoration on their clothing, from the simple to the elaborate. A close study of the clothing of any period will not only show the values and customs of that time, but the materials that were available and the tools or implements that were used.

Needlework, in all its forms, expresses beauty as well as emotion; it reflects more accurately, the period. Whether needlework enhances clothing, or decorates the home, it can be a powerful form of self-expression. It is therefore believed to be a true mirror of the culture, tradition, philosophy, and lifestyle of the time during which it was created. It is a piece of beauty—a work of art.

Throughout history, the development of needlework has been as widespread and varied as the works themselves. Russia and Italy developed the cross stitch, Spain, the outline stitch. From Madeira came drawnwork, and from the Scots came the woven plaid. Scandinavia produced the hooked coverlets and rugs, while the American Indian gave us beaded work. Every culture has produced their own type and form of needlework, the only exception is America. Instead, with the exchange of techniques, patterns, designs and materials, what has developed is a collage of many different patterns; it is a very unique style of needlework. What is now considered "American" is actually a very special blend of influences from many different cultures. For example, in European societies there had been definite class distinctions in needlework, the "gentlewoman" did fine embroidery while the lower class woman did "folk art" or plain seamstress work. However, in American society these were combined to produce a new type of needlework with a style all its own. As diverse as its population, American needlework is truly a reflection of its unique culture.

Since sewing and needlework have traditionally been the work of women, it can be said that here has been no other tangible art form which has expressed their individuality and their creativity as well. Whether done to decorate the home, to please a child or for a feeling of accomplishment, needlework has always been a medium of self-expression. In every form, this expression of creativity and ingenuity is very personal, and will always carry with it a part of its creators. It is art to be admired and cherished.

How to Use This Book

๛๛๛๛๛๛๛๛๛๛

Each category represents a tool or implement used in sewing and needlework. The categories are arranged alphabetically and offer a full description of each item. When possible, a brief history is given.

The additional categories of paper and advertising collectibles are included. These items represent a new trend in sewing and needlework collectibles and can certainly add color and charm to any collection.

PRICE NOTES

This book was written as a buyer's price guide. The prices reported in this book are the prices a buyer can expect to pay for a particular item, not the price at which the collector can expect to sell. In order to determine the value of a particular item, an average was taken from prices gathered from dealers, auctions, antique and collectibles shows, flea markets, collectors clubs and related magazines and periodicals. Throughout this guide, unless otherwise noted, prices are based on items that are in excellent condition. It is safe to assume that any item showing a substantial amount of use or wear would be priced accordingly. It is unfortunate, but necessary, to note that since most sewing and needlework items were used on a consistent basis it is usually difficult to find pieces in mint condition.

Prices that have been reported are of items that are recognized antiques, as well as those items considered to be collectibles. An item is considered an antique if it has attained a venerable age, is no longer produced or is not popularly used. Therefore, the price quoted for these particular items usually reflects a more accurate picture of the value of that piece. Spinning wheels, Shaker items, yarn winders, store cabinets and chatelaines are good examples of items that are usually quite old, are no longer in production, or are being made on a limited, well identified reproduction basis. They are recognized antiques with relatively well established prices.

On the other hand, when dealing with the collectibles market, prices tend to vary more because items are relatively new and abundant. Good examples of items found in the collectibles market are needle books, rulers, trade cards, magazines, and catalogs. For a nominal price, many of these items can be found at flea markets as well as local garage and household sales. Remember, until you do find a piece that interests you, rummaging through all these available items can be half the fun.

No matter what you are looking for, or where you look, one must venture into any marketplace with cautious optimism. Keep in mind that many sewing and needlework tools have been made of the same material and in the same design over the centuries. The collector must do some research to determine if an item is truly as valuable as it appears to be. Also, as you travel throughout the country, always visit local

auctions, antique shows and flea markets to become knowl-
edgeable as to an item's availability and collectibility in that
particular area. Finally, remember to always have a good
time!

Bodkins

The word bodkin actually refers to four very different objects. Besides its meaning in sewing and needlework, it can also refer to a dagger, an ornamental hairpin or a punch (stiletto). For our purpose, bodkin refers to an implement for drawing ribbon, cord or tape through holes or casings in fabric. It looks like a fat needle with a blunt rounded end and an elongated eye that is big enough for the ribbon to be passed through. Throughout the ages bodkins have not changed appreciably in appearance. They have usually been made of ivory, mother-of-pearl, silver, silver plate, brass or steel.

Bodkins are listed alphabetically by the material of which they are made.

See "Punches."

CURRENT
PRICE

BONE

☐ Plain, 3″		6.00
☐ Turned top, 3½″		7.00

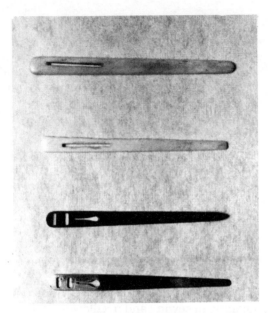

Bodkins. *Top to bottom.* Ivory, 3⅜″, $8.00; bone, 3″, $6.00; brass, 3″, $1.00; steel, 3″, $1.50.

CURRENT
PRICE

IVORY

☐ Whale, two elaborately carved outside sections, with four carved openwork columns in the center 350.00

MOTHER-OF-PEARL

☐ Plain, 3″ 12.00

STEEL

☐ Plain, 2¼″ 3.00

STERLING SILVER

☐ Art Deco decoration 30.00
☐ Chased, Victorian 25.00
☐ Embossed, ornate floral decoration, set of
    three 55.00
☐ Engraved, floral decoration, hallmarked 25.00
☐ Fish-shape tops, set of three in silk case 65.00
☐ Fish-shape tops, set of two and one turned
    bone, original box 50.00
☐ Plain, set of three, graduated sizes 45.00
☐ Plain 22.00
☐ Relief floral decoration, hallmarked 27.00

SCRIMSHAW

☐ Folding, triple 55.00

WHALE BONE

☐ Carved hand at top, circa 1860s, $4\frac{7}{8}$ " 130.00
☐ Carved, set of four, circa 1850 .... 290.00

WOOD

☐ Yew, plain in yew burl box with inlaid edges,
    circa 1790s, $3\frac{1}{4}$ " 130.00

Buttonhole Cutters, Buttonhole Scissors and Seam Cutters

❀❀❀❀❀❀❀❀❀❀❀

Buttonhole cutters, buttonhole scissors and seam cutters (also known as seam rippers or seam knives) can all perform the same tasks. They can be used to cut a buttonhole as well as cut apart a seam.

Buttonhole cutters were used mostly during the eighteenth and nineteenth centuries. They are simply small metal tools with a sharp, sliding knife attached.

Buttonhole scissors are best described as specific types of small scissors that are adjustable by a screw and ratchet mechanism. The adjustable mechanism allows the scissors to be set to start the cut at a specific distance (up to ½ inch) from the edge of the fabric.

Originally, the seam cutter had a spade-shaped blade usually made of steel or iron attached to a handle of wood, bone, ivory, or metal. These were made with the blade placed

Advertising combination buttonhole cutter, seam ripper, needle threader. Green metal case, 3⅝" long, $15.00.

at a right angle to the handle. Later, the seam cutter was made with an unbalanced U-shaped end. The longer side of the U is pointed, the bottom of the U is sharp and the short side of the U has a guard-covered end. This type of seam cutter is still being made and can probably be found in the sewing basket or box of the present day needleworker.

CURRENT
PRICE

BUTTONHOLE CUTTERS

☐ Cambridge Cutlery Co., Germany, 4¾" 30.00
☐ Iron, hand-forged blade, bone handle, circa
   1825, 3" 80.00
☐ Iron, hand-forged blade, iron handle, circa
   1820, 3" 65.00
☐ Iron, hand-forged blade, wooden knob-shaped
   handle, 3½" 75.00
☐ Iron, two hand-forged blades placed at right
   angle to flat faceted handle, 18th century 90.00
☐ Roger's Shear Co., 1776, Germany, 4" 25.00

Buttonhole scissors. Bayonne Knife Co., NJ, screw pivot, 4⅝" long, $16.00.

BUTTONHOLE SCISSORS

CURRENT
PRICE

☐ Nickle-plated steel, with inside set screws,
4½" 15.00
☐ Steel, marked "Germany," 4½" 15.00
☐ Steel, with one adjustable thumbscrew 12.00
☐ Unknown metal, with attached round wheel,
marked "Butterick" 40.00

SEAM CUTTERS

☐ Iron, hand-wrought 18.00
☐ Ivory, figural Buddha 22.00
☐ Mother-of-pearl, small 30.00
☐ Steel 12.00

Seam ripper with removable end caps. "Rip 'n Pik" in raised letters on red plastic case, 1¼" measure on case, $2.50.

Buttons

No one really knows when or where buttons were first used on clothing. Originally, they were probably made and worn as ornaments. By the sixteenth century buttons were an important part of most items of clothing. By the eighteenth century they were playing an important role in fashion; buttons became larger, were available in many varieties and were now extensively used on clothing. Button manufacture in America did not begin on any major scale until after the Revolutionary War. At first, only buttons that were necessary, made of materials at hand, were produced. Almost all of the finer buttons had to be imported.

Buttons absolutely abound. They can be found everywhere, and in many varieties. The different sizes, shapes, colors, designs, and materials used are astonishing. For this very reason, buttons are undoubtedly one of the easiest objects to start collecting. Every house has at least a few buttons tucked away, so even a beginning collector may be pleasantly surprised to find that their collection is off to a fine start. The best place to begin searching for buttons is in the household button box. It will not take a great deal of rummaging through the box to discover the many wonderful types of buttons that can be found, an activity which also provides many hours of enjoyment.

Most of the buttons that can be found on the market today are from the last half of the nineteenth century and early twentieth century. Collecting these buttons can be great fun and relatively inexpensive. Buttons can be found at auctions, antique shows and shops, flea markets and house sales. But be aware that you may have to ask for buttons in many antique shops, as they do not always have them on display. Another way to enhance any collection is by trading the buttons you already have. To be in touch with other button collectors attend button club meetings and specialized button shows held throughout the country. Dedicated button collectors have done extensive research on the history of buttons and have done a tremendous job of identifying and categorizing buttons. Visiting with these people can be very informative and quite enjoyable.

A novice collector typically starts by collecting all types of buttons. Eventually, the collector will begin to specialize as personal preferences begin to develop. Button collectors will often categorize their collection according to material, construction or design, to name a few. But perhaps the most exciting part of button collecting is its potential to inform. An added bonus to button collecting is that inevitably it will lead to reading and researching history, costume design and literature—and these are only a few of the fascinating areas that may be explored.

Definitions of a few terms:

Sew through, button with holes for the thread that will attach it to the fabric.

Pearl buttons on original card. France, baby size, $6.00;
brass button in basketweave pattern, ⅞″ diameter, $1.50;
pearl button with diagonal cuts, brass back, ¾″ diameter.
$1.25.

Shank, the means by which a button with no holes can
    be attached to the fabric.

Self-shank, or one-piece button, the shank is all in one
    piece with the button. It has a drilled hole.

Metal shank, metal piece set into the back of the button.

Loop shank, wire or metal in the shape of a loop set into
    the back of the button.

Collet, the metal rim that holds a set jewel.

Rim, the setting or border of a button.

The categories that follow concentrate on those buttons
made during the late 1800s and early 1900s. Because this
time frame has been chosen, many of the buttons described
should be available on the market today.

BONE

Bone buttons have been used since the middle of the sixteenth century. They were made from skeletons of domestic

Top. Brown, gold and black hand painted, 7/8″ diameter, $ .55. *Bottom left.* Simulated leather, 5/8″ diameter, $ .40. *Bottom right.* Natural, advertising, 11/16″ diameter, $ .20.

animals and deer, and were considered the common person's answer to ivory buttons. They were less expensive but also not made nearly as well, as tool marks are often apparent on these early buttons. The majority of bone buttons were plain and came in sizes from approximately one-quarter inch to a little over one inch in diameter. There are a few bone buttons that can be found that are decorated by carvings, paintings, piercings, and used in combination with other materials. Decorated bone buttons date from the middle of the eighteenth century to the late nineteenth century. Bone has also been used for inlays on other buttons (in imitation of ivory) and as backing for other buttons.

Bone buttons have been made as two hole, three hole, or four hole sew-through buttons, with self-shanks and metal shanks. They were used on all types of clothing. In particular, many of the sew-through buttons were made to be used on underwear.

Bone buttons are listed alphabetically by decoration.

CURRENT
PRICE

ABALONE

☐ Bone and abalone inlay, two hole, oval 1.35

CURRENT
PRICE

BRASS

☐ Bone base with chased brass center disk,
   metal shank, 1″ diameter 1.00
☐ Bone base with embedded brass ring, ¹³/₁₆″
   diameter .... .75

CARVED

☐ Book carved in base, ½″ × ¾″ 1.25
☐ Line design in center, pierced border, metal
   shank, ⅞″ diameter .... .75
☐ Line design, self-shank, ⅞″ diameter .... .70
☐ Flower carved in base and painted, 1″
   diameter .... .90
☐ Flowers carved in base in high relief, copper
   rim and back, 1⅛″ diameter 1.75

PEARL

☐ Bone base with gold tracery and pearl
   inlay, ⅝″ diameter 1.35
☐ Bone base with pearl set in center, 1″ diameter 1.25

PIERCED

☐ All-over pierced, self-shank, ⅞″ diameter 1.45
☐ Two arrangements of three holes, sew
   through, ⅞″ diameter .... .50
☐ Two arrangements of five holes, sew through,
   ¹¹/₁₆″ diameter .... .60

PLAIN

☐ Four hole sew through, rim .... .20
☐ Two large holes, underwear button .... .20
☐ Nailhead on face, pin turns into shank, ¾″
   and 1⅛″ diameter .... .40
☐ Narrow self rim, four hole sew through, ½″
   diameter .... .20

STEEL

☐ Bone base with circular steel mirrors, ½"
diameter 1.25
☐ Bone base with oval steel mirrors, ⅝"
diameter 1.25

BRASS

Brass buttons have been made since the sixteenth century and have always been made in great quantities. Brass has always been a very satisfactory material for buttons as it is durable, easy to cast or stamp, plate and gild. Brass could easily be used in combination with other materials. All types of materials such as ivory, bone, pearl, glass, steel, etc., could be set into brass.

The first brass buttons were cast in a single piece. A projecting portion was cast on the back and was drilled with a hole after removal from the cast. This was a one-piece button with a self-shank. Some cast buttons had applied shanks which were usually wire loops.

By 1790 the process of rolling brass in sheets had been improved and production became easier and more economical. Gold plating had become the fashion and picture buttons were very popular. Rolled brass could easily be stamped with any design. By 1823 two-piece buttons were invented and brass buttons quickly adapted to this style.

Brass buttons have been made in a vast array of designs and variety of sizes. They are still being made and are popularly used. Brass buttons are probably the most popular type of button to collect. A collector of brass buttons should take the time to do some reading on the subject, as many of the buttons have specific names which identify the design. The names have historical, mythological or literary importance.

Left. Pearl center set in brass, 1¹⁵/₁₆″ diameter, $2.50. *Top.* Brass stamped design of shield and eagles in relief, ³/₄″ diameter, $ .85. *Bottom.* Brass stamped floral design on mirror back, ⁷/₈″ diameter, $1.75.

Please note that military brass buttons have been omitted, as they are a complex group and should be studied in more depth than a book of this size would allow.

Brass buttons are listed alphabetically by the decoration. See also the other button categories (pearl, glass, etc.) for brass buttons in combination with other materials.

CURRENT
PRICE

ANIMALS

☐ Bear, teddy, stamped design, circa 1907, ⁷/₈″
  diameter 4.50
☐ Bear, teddy, stamped design with inscription,
  "Will You Be My Teddy Bear," encircling
  bear, two-piece, ⁹/₁₆″ diameter 5.00
☐ Bee, stamped design in high relief, concave
  base 2.25
☐ Bird, sitting on branch, stamped design,
  stamped design on rim, two-piece, ⁵/₈″
  diameter 1.50

☐ Bird, Phoenix, die-cut design, brass back, 1¾″
diameter 6.50

☐ Boar, wild, stamped design of charging boar,
black composition back, ¾″ diameter, scarce 16.00

☐ Buffalo, trampling dog with another dog chasing a hare in background, stamped design,
high convex shape with tin back, brass shank,
1″ diameter 20.00

☐ Bull's head in silhouette, stamped design in
high relief, silvered, brass shank 5.00

☐ Bullfight scene, stamped design of picador on
horse fending off bull, pierced brass, collet,
brass shank, several sizes 1.25

☐ Cat in flowered bonnet, stamped design in
high relief, 1⅛″ diameter 9.50

☐ Cat in vines with butterflies above, stamped
design, 1½″ diameter 3.50

☐ Cat, head etched on palette, brushes and palette in low relief, stippled background, one-
piece, brass shank, ¹⁵/₁₆″ diameter 4.00

☐ Cat, head and paws stamped design in high
relief, pierced background over mirror back,
brass shank, 2½″ diameter 8.50

☐ Cat, head, full face in silhouette, high relief,
green brilliant eyes, brass shank 8.00

☐ Cat, head, snarling with forepaws showing,
high relief on plain concave button, flat brass
shank, 1″ diameter 9.50

☐ Cat, timid, breaking through paper, high relief, scalloped edge with depressions painted
dark green, one-piece, brass shank, ⅞″
diameter 8.00

☐ Cat, Cheshire, face with laurel foilage background, stamped design, tin back, brass
shank, ¹⁵/₁₆″ diameter 14.00

☐ Cow, stamped design with inscription, "Cow hide Brand Overalls," ¾" diameter 2.50

☐ Cow looking over fence, trees on both sides, stamped design, two-piece, brass shank, ¾" diameter 2.25

☐ Deer, stamped and tinted design, two-piece, ⅝" diameter 2.00

☐ Deer, head, in high relief, two-piece, self-shank, ⅝" to ⅞" diameter 3.25

☐ Dog, stamped design in relief, two-piece, ¾" diameter 6.00

☐ Dog surrounded by wreath, pierced design superimposed, tinted concave background, ⁹⁄₁₆" diameter 7.50

☐ Dragon, head with crown, stamped design, one-piece, 1" diameter 5.00

☐ Elephant, stamped design in high relief, ¾" diameter 7.50

☐ Fox, running, stamped design, 1¼" diameter . 2.50

☐ Frog and Rabbit, stamped design, Aesop's Fable 21.00

☐ Horse and rider with dog, stamped design, tin back, 1⅛" diameter 5.00

☐ Horse and rider jumping fence, stamped design, ⅞" diameter 2.00

☐ Horse, head, stamped design in high relief, textured background, two-piece, 1" to 1½" diameter 2.25

☐ Kittens and basket, one kitten in basket, one out, brass on pearl, ¾" diameter 5.75

☐ Lion, head, stamped design in high relief, one-piece 2.00

☐ Ostrich, stamped design, velvet background, ⅝" diameter 1.00

☐ Owl, head, steel eyes and steel back, ¾" 8.00

☐ Rooster, stamped design, two-piece 11.00

☐ Squirrels, stamped design, two-piece, various
sizes .... .50

☐ Stork, stamped design, two-piece, wire shank,
³/₄ " diameter 2.75

☐ Swan, stamped design on concave button,
two-piece, ⁹/₁₆ " diameter 2.50

☐ Wildcat, four heads, cut steel cross separation
of heads, one-piece, brass shank, ¹/₂ " diameter 1.50

☐ Wildcat, four heads, surrounding design set
with steel, brass shank, 1³/₈ " diameter 1.50

FLORALS

☐ All-over floral chased design, two-piece, gilt,
1¹/₈ " diameter 1.45

☐ All-over floral design on color background,
two-piece, various sizes .... .50

☐ All-over floral design in relief, soldered to face,
one-piece, 1 " diameter 1.00

☐ All-over pierced floral design, colored back,
two-piece, various sizes .... .50

☐ Basket with flowers, pierced design, tinted
background, one-piece, ³/₄ " to 1¹/₈ " diameter ... 1.25

☐ Basket with flowers, stamped design, two-
piece, various sizes .... .50

☐ Basket with flowers, stamped design, tinted
background, 1¹/₈ " diameter .... .60

☐ Basket with flowers, superimposed design,
steel studded, various sizes .... .75

☐ Child's head in flowers, stamped design in relief, two-piece, wire shank, 1 " diameter 2.00

☐ Chrysanthemum, pierced design, blue-green
trim, ⁷/₈ " diameter 1.25

☐ Hat with flowers, stamped design, colored
background, 1³/₄ " diameter 1.45

☐ Floral pattern units around edge, incised design, convex, 1″ diameter 2.00

☐ Flowerpot, stamped design in low relief, one-piece, 1¼″ diameter 3.00

☐ Flowers in urn, stamped design superimposed on flat base, steel faceted rim, 1½″ diameter .. 6.00

☐ Oriental vase with flowers, stamped design, tinted, cone shank, ¹⁵/₁₆″ diameter 3.50

☐ Rose, stamped design, leaf border, engraved detail, 1⅛″ diameter 1.50

☐ Rosebud, stamped design, enamel detail, ¼″ diameter 1.75

☐ Tulips, stamped design 1.40

☐ Tulips, stamped design attached to steel back, etched edge, 1½″ diameter 5.00

☐ Water Lily, stamped and pierced design, enamel touches 8.50

HANDS

☐ Left hand, stamped design in relief, berries with open work centers show mirror back, two-piece, brass shank, ½″ diameter 4.50

☐ Left hand holding rose, stamped design in relief, self-shank, ½″ diameter 2.00

☐ Left hand holding spray of cut steel fruit, stamped design, tinted, brass shank, 9¹/₆″ diameter 2.25

☐ Left hand wearing wedding ring and holding cut steel studded cherries, stamped design, brass shank, ⁹/₁₆″ diameter 4.30

☐ Right hand, incised design, two-piece, brass shank, ¼″ diameter 5.00

☐ Right hand, wrist set with cut steels, black composition, escutcheon background, steel back, wire shank, ½″ diameter 3.25

☐ Right hand, stamped design, wrist set with
cut steels, smoked pearl center, repousse border of polished steel, brass shank, 1⅛"
diameter 6.00

☐ Right hand and arm with hammer, stamped
design in low relief with inscription, "Mechan-
ics Garments," ¾" diameter 1.00

☐ Right hand and arm with hammer, stamped
design in relief superimposed in two-piece
metal, ⅞" diameter 1.25

☐ Right hand and bird holding letter, stamped
design, gray background, brass collet and
shank, 9/16" diameter 7.50

☐ Right hand and bird perched on little
finger, stamped design, double ruffle, brass
shank, 1" diameter 7.25

☐ Right hand holding acanthus, design in relief,
one-piece, ⅜" diameter 1.75

☐ Right hand holding carnation, stamped design
on engraved background, two-piece, brass
shank, ½" diameter 6.75

☐ Right hand holding fan, stamped design, self-
shank, ½" diameter 1.50

☐ Right hand holding flower, stamped design,
stippled background, two-piece, self-shank 1.50

☐ Right hand holding flower, ruffle at wrist,
blackened tin rim and background, wire
shank, 1⅞" diameter 2.50

☐ Right hand holding flower, ruffle at wrist,
darkened background, raised engraved edge,
brass shank, 1⅜" diameter 2.75

☐ Right hand holding flower with cut steel center, one-piece steel, wire shank, ½" diameter .. 1.85

☐ Right hand holding flowers, stamped design in
high relief, brass shank, ½" diameter 3.00

☐ Right hand holding flowers on smokey pearl background, wire shank, $9/16''$ diameter 4.50

☐ Right hand holding roses, stamped design, dark stippled background, tin collet, brass shank, $1\frac{1}{2}''$ diameter 2.65

☐ Right hand holding wreath, design in relief, blackened tin background, brass collet, self–shank, $\frac{1}{2}$ diameter 3.50

☐ Right hand with embroidered cuff holding flowers, design in high relief on flat base, brass shank, $1\frac{5}{8}''$ diameter 3.75

☐ Right hand wearing glove holding flowers, design in high relief on flat background, brass shank, $\frac{5}{8}''$ diameter 2.75

☐ Right hand with sword, "Excalibur," pierced design in high relief, dark background, tin collet, brass shank, $1\frac{1}{16}''$ diameter 13.00

VARIOUS DESIGNS

☐ Acorn and leaf, stamped design, steel cup, rim and back, $1\frac{1}{8}''$ diameter .... .50

☐ Airplane (early), stamped design, two-piece, $13/16''$ diameter .... .50

☐ Anchor, stamped design, convex, self-shank ... .40

☐ Anchor, stamped design, two-piece, $\frac{1}{2}''$ diameter .... .40

☐ Anchor, stamped design, stippled background, two-piece, $\frac{5}{8}''$ diameter .... .40

☐ Anchor, stars around rim, two-piece, convex, gilt-lined background, $15/16''$ diameter .... .75

☐ Anchor with rope, stamped design in high relief, tin back, $1\frac{1}{8}''$ diameter .... .50

☐ Anchor with rope, stamped design, one-piece, two-hole, various sizes .... .40

☐ Anchor with flower and rope, stamped design, polished steel background .... .40

☐ Anchor, relief design surrounded by circles in
chain, 1″ diameter .... .50

☐ Automobile, stamped early car design in relief,
stamped brass cone, metal loop shank, ½″ to
1¾″ diameter 1.25

☐ Ax, steel in center, faceted steel on rim, one-
piece, ⅞″ diameter 1.50

☐ Basketweave, stamped design, ½″ diameter ... .40

☐ Bow, superimposed on steel back, ⅝″
diameter 1.00

☐ Buckle and strap, design in relief, one-piece,
tinted, 1⅛″ diameter 1.50

☐ Cherubs with cornucopia and goat, stamped
design 6.50

☐ Clock, stamped design with raised numerals
and hands, two-piece, 1″ diameter 2.25

☐ Club (card deck), stamped design with inscription "Black Glass Club," ½″ diameter 1.75

☐ Crown, stamped design in relief, two-piece,
1⅛″ diameter 1.25

☐ Cupid at Rest, stamped design, steel rim 8.50

☐ Dice, stamped design, tinted, two-piece, ½″
diameter 1.50

☐ Drum, stamped design in relief, 1″ diameter .. 1.75

☐ Ewer, stamped design in relief surrounded by
scroll design, two-piece, ⅞″ diameter 2.25

☐ Ewer, stamped design surrounded by scroll
design, one-piece, tinted, ⅝″ diameter 2.50

☐ Fan, stamped and pierced design, cut steel
border, 9⁄16″ diameter 1.00

☐ Fishline and hook, stamped design, wire-mesh
background, solid rim 1.25

☐ Fleur-de-lis, pierced brass design, one-piece,
tinted, various sizes 1.50

☐ Fruit, stamped design in relief, two-piece, 11⁄16″
and 1⅛″ 1.75

☐ Garden of Eden, stamped design 16.00

CURRENT
PRICE

☐ Gay Nineties, stamped design, filigree border, cobalt glass center, 1¾″ 4.00

☐ Golf clubs and ball, stamped design in relief, two-piece, ½″ diameter .... .75

☐ Halley's Comet, stamped design, engraved stars on black background, 1⅛″ 5.50

☐ Hat and Umbrella, stamped design in relief, two-piece, ⅝″ diameter 1.00

☐ Heart, stamped design in relief, convex, one-piece, ⅜″ diameter 1.00

☐ Hunting horn, stamped design, one-piece, separate rim, ½″ diameter 1.00

☐ Key and Keyhole, stamped and pierced design, pebbled background, one-piece, brass shank, ¾″ diameter 1.25

☐ Keys, stamped design in relief, brass shank, ¹¹/₁₆″ diameter 1.00

☐ Knocker, steel attached to figured brass button, brass shank, ¾″ diameter 1.50

☐ Leaf, stamped border design on dotted background, one-piece, ⅝″ diameter .... .80

☐ Leaf, stamped design, tinted, one-piece, 1″ diameter .... .75

☐ Leaf, holly, stamped design in relief, ¾″ to 1¼ diameter 1.25

☐ Liberty Bell, stamped and pierced design in relief, impressed "1776" in cut-out, two-piece, 1″ diameter 1.25

☐ Locomotive, stamped design of locomotive on bridge, boatman in rowboat below, one-piece, tinted, ⅝″ diameter 2.00

☐ Lohengrin, stamped design in high relief, celluloid background, ⅝″ diameter 3.75

☐ Oriental scene, stamped design of man and woman, mulberry background, 1⅛″ diameter 3.00

☐ Oriental scene, stamped design of palms, boat, and buildings, tin back, 1″ diameter 2.75

☐ Padlock, pierced design, brass shank, ¾″ diameter .... .80

☐ Padlock. pierced design, mounted in brass ring, brass shank, ¾″ diameter 1.50

☐ Padlock in imitation of handbag, dark background, brass collet and shank, ¾″ diameter .. 2.00

☐ Padlock, stamped design, inscription, brass shank, ¹³⁄₁₆″ diameter 1.00

☐ Pierrot and Pierrette, stamped design, textured cup base, white metal moon 3.50

☐ Plain with mesh center, 1¼″ 2.00

☐ Pomegranate, stamped design, tinted, one-piece, 1″ diameter .... .75

☐ Powder horn, stamped design in relief, two-piece, ⅝″ diameter .... .75

☐ Sail boat and sea gulls, stamped design, one-piece, wire shank, ⅝″ diameter 1.00

☐ Sailing ship, stamped design, tinted, two-piece, ¾″ diameter .... .80

☐ Sailing ship and lighthouse, stamped design, two-piece, various sizes .... .50

☐ Shield, stamped design, steel-studded shield, set in steel cup, 1½″ diameter 1.50

☐ Stairway to palace, stamped pattern, two-piece, wire shank, ⁹⁄₁₆″ diameter 1.00

☐ Strawberries, stamped design, filigree border, two-piece 2.25

☐ Tree, stamped and pierced design in relief, ¹⁵⁄₁₆″ diameter 1.25

☐ Trophy, stamped design, two-piece, tinted, 1⅛″ and 1¼″ .... .75

☐ Utah State Seal, beehive stamped design, convex, ⅞″ diameter 1.50

CURRENT
PRICE

☐ Woman on bicycle, stamped design superimposed on iridescent pearl background, 1⅛″
diameter 3.50

☐ Yum-Yum (Mikado), stamped design, tinted,
engraved detail, ½″ diameter 1.75

☐ Zodiac signs, stamped brass design in relief,
metal shank, ⅝″ 1.25

CELLULOID

Celluloid first appeared as a practical material in 1869. It was
used as a substitution for ivory, wood, pearl, black glass and
hard rubber in producing a vast array of items. Celluloid is
the first commercial plastic. It is very hard, resists moisture
and can be highly polished. The earliest celluloid buttons had
celluloid backgrounds and were set in brass. Many buttons
in the Art Nouveau and Art Deco style were manufactured.

Celluloid can be tested by applying a hot needle; it will
give off an odor of camphor and a hiss. Remember to always
test in a very inconspicuous place on the item.

Celluloid buttons are listed alphabetically by type of decoration.

CURRENT
PRICE

BRASS

☐ Anchor, superimposed on celluloid base, ⅜″
diameter 1.25

COLORED

☐ Black celluloid with metal center strip, 1¼″ ×
2″ 30

☐ Black and gray celluloid halves divided by
metal, 1″ × 1″ 20

☐ Pink celluloid with off-center white trim, 1″
diameter .... .20

FIGURAL

☐ Ball shape, red with slots in top, ⅞″ diameter   .25
☐ Drum shape, black and white stripes, ⅞″
diameter .... .20
☐ Drum shape, brown with white metal off-
center trim, ¾″ diameter .... .20
☐ Half-barrel shaped, looks like wood, 1¼″
long .... .30
☐ Leaf shape, green, 1″ long .... .20
☐ Well shape with round fabric button set in,
tortoise color, 1¾″ diameter 1.00

JEWEL

☐ Clear color celluloid to imitate clear glass,
paste jewels in rim, 1″ diameter .... .45
☐ Imitation pearl, six celluloid pearls on metal
base, ⅞″ diameter .... .35

PLAIN

☐ Round with two large sew-through holes, pearl
finish, 1″ diameter .... .30

PICTURE

☐ Aviator and plane, polycrome print under
celluloid .... .35
☐ Camel, stamped design on high-domed black
celluloid bubble, ⅞″ diameter 2.75
☐ Chair, polycrome print under celluloid, gilt
rim, ½″ diameter .... .45
☐ Floral bouquet, stamped design, brass rim,
brass back, 1½″ diameter 6.50

CURRENT
PRICE

- ☐ Floral, stamped design in black, pink and blue, pasteboard filling, tin back, 1⁵⁄₁₆″ diameter 2.35
- ☐ Floral, stamped design, large central flower surrounded by small flowers, cream color, 1″ square .... .40
- ☐ Floral, stamped design, imitation sandwich glass, 1¼″ diameter .... .25
- ☐ Fox and Grapes, stamped design on tan disc in high relief, 1⁵⁄₈″ diameter 1.50
- ☐ Horse and Rider, stamped design, printed surface design, metal back, ¹⁵⁄₁₆″ diameter 1.25
- ☐ Locomotive, stamped design, high dome, antique finish, modern .... .40
- ☐ Polo player, stamped design, one-piece, circa 1930, 1½″ diameter 2.75
- ☐ Star, celluloid with glass insert, metal edge simulating cut steel, ¾″ diameter .... .85

CHINA

This term, which seems to be the present-day designation, when applied to buttons, is very confusing as it seems to embrace all clay products that are made into a form and then fired. This would include all chinas, porcelains, bone chinas, stoneware, delft, majolica, ceramics, and parian ware. When referred to in books on buttons, the terms get intermingled and come out as one type. There is no, or little, differentiation between porcelain, bisque, ceramic or any other type. They all mean a type of fired clay product that is not transparent or translucent.

We have known how to make ceramics since 4,000 B.C. and many useful items have been made and decorated since that time. When China buttons were first made is not known. What we do know, is that once they began to be produced, they were decorated in many ways. They could be etched, carved, hand-painted or molded, to name a few. Today, China buttons are still being made but mainly with transfer or molded decorations.

China buttons are listed alphabetically by type of decoration.

CURRENT
PRICE

BENNINGTON

☐ Metal setting 2.50

BRASS

☐ Classical head in opaque white china, metal
    shank 1.00
☐ Fluted ring around center, four-hole sew
    through .... .85
☐ Single large ring around center, two-hole sew
    through .... .85

JEWEL

☐ Black star inlaid in blue china, brass base 2.50

MOLDED

☐ Floral design, self-shrank, unglazed back,
    1³/₁₆″ diameter 1.90
☐ Floral design in relief, painted in polychrome,
    glazed disc, 1¹/₈″ diameter 1.75

PAINTED

☐ Anchor, hand-painted 18.00
☐ Bird, hand-painted 28.00
☐ Bird with branch in beak, hand-painted, scal-
    loped border 37.00
☐ Blue painted with silver deposit decoration,
    glazed body, self-shank, ⁷/₈″ diameter 5.00
☐ Fruit, hand-painted, not signed, modern 2.50
☐ Garlands, hand-painted, signed, modern 8.50

CURRENT
PRICE

☐ Pink and white stripes painted on convex but-
ton, brass base 1.75
☐ Wild roses, Meissen, hand-painted and signed 65.00

PLAIN

☐ Bull's eye, metal shank, various sizes .... .25
☐ Fisheye, orange, two-hole sew through .... .30
☐ Round, black-banded, metal shank, 1″
diameter .... .30
☐ Round, four-hole sew through, 7/8″ diameter ... .30
☐ Round, green with gilt and silver luster .... .60
☐ Round with initial in silver luster, white,
metal shank .... .65
☐ Round with pie crust trim, 1/2″ diameter .... .25
☐ Round with spatter decoration, 3/4″ .... .40
☐ Three rings, two-hole sew through .... .40

STENCIL

☐ Pattern #12, ivory glazed body, two-hole sew
through, various colors and sizes .... .35
☐ Pattern #29, black face, 1840-1940, 9/16″
diameter 1.25

TERRA-COTTA

☐ Brown and mazarine blue, metal shank, 1¼″
diameter 1.50
☐ Brown and red trim, sew through, various
sizes .... .60
☐ Brown and tan, glazed, brass pin through cen-
ter turns into shank, various sizes .... .50
☐ Mottled brown and tan, glazed, 1″ diameter ... .75
☐ Mottled brown and tan, glazed, rimmed, 1″
diameter .... .75

TRANSFER

☐ Calico, three-hole sew through .... .50

☐ Calico, metal setting, four-hole sew through ... 1.50

☐ Calico, metal setting, metal shank, 1″
diameter 1.50

☐ Calico, rounded rim, depressed holes and cen-
ter, ⅝″ diameter .... .90

☐ Cards in polychrome design, self-shank, black
background and back, 1¼″ .... .85

☐ Daisy in polychrome design, black background, metal back, 1½″ diameter 1.45

☐ Face in monochrome design, various sizes ...... .40

☐ Floral in polychrome design, self-shank, circa
19th century, ½″ diameter 7.50

☐ Floral in polychrome design, gold outlining
and incrustation, self-shank, various sizes 1.00

☐ Floral in polychrome design, metal body with
basketweave design, 1⅛″ diameter 1.45

☐ Gingham in red and green design, various
sizses .... .45

☐ Man kneeling with bow scene, black and white
on maroon background, self-shank, painted
gold rim, 1¼″ diameter 1.85

☐ Paisley in blues, gilt-stamped rim, four-way
shank 1.25

☐ Paisley in polychrome design, glazed disc,
metal back, 1⁵⁄₁₆″ diameter 1.10

☐ Roses, pink and green leaves design, convex
white china base 1.75

☐ Sailing ship in polychrome design, on glazed
ceramic disc, painted gold rim, self-shank 1.00

☐ Sunburst in monochrome design, rim, center
jewel, ½″ diameter .... .75

- ☐ Wavy lines in colors on white body, 1″
  diameter .... .35
- ☐ Zodiac figures in polychrome design, black let-
  tering, rims, 1⅛″ diameter .... .60
- ☐ Zodiac signs in four colors on white china,
  self-shank, various sizes .... .50

ENAMEL

The art of enamel work has been done for many centuries. Certainly Byzantine enamelling was at its best in 800 A.D. Some form of enamelling has continued throughout the ages. There are three major types of enamel work.

> *Cloisonne* is the earliest form. Very fine metal bands were laid out on the base metal in the projected design. Finely powdered glass was turned into a paste form and applied between the bands. This was then fired until the glass melted. The piece was then highly polished. Designs were very intricate and very highly skilled craftsmen executed the pieces. Glass could be used as the base, but more often they were of metal.
>
> *Champlete* was developed as a simpler method of Cloisonne. Depressions were made in the base metal or glass, then filled with enamel, fired, and polished.
>
> *Painted* is the form that is most commonly found today. The design is painted on a smooth enamel background with fine brushes, using enamel colors. The piece is then fire-polished.

During the nineteenth and twentieth centuries, enamel work has been widely manufactured in America, Europe and the Orient. Most buttons found on the market today will be from this time period and of the painted type.

Enamel buttons are listed alphabetically by the type of decoration.

☐ Anchor in brass and pierced red enamel shield, set in steel cup, ½″ diameter, modern .   1.00

☐ Art Deco with stylized florals, painted in polychrome enamels, faceted steel border, 1⅜″ diameter 8.00

☐ Basket design, painted in polychrome enamels, ornate gilt rim, 1″ diameter 12.00

☐ Boats and harbor design, painted in polychrome enamel design on enamel, steel-studded rim, ¾″ diameter 2.50

☐ Book design, painted in polychrome enamel design, ¾″ diameter 1.50

☐ Ewer design, painted in polychrome enamel design, ornamental rim, ¾″ diameter 3.00

☐ Floral brass and polychrome enamel design center on black background, faceted steels set in border, 1¼″ diameter 14.00

☐ Floral with rosebud on white enamel shield, ⅜″ diameter 3.00

☐ Floral with rosebud in cobalt enamel border, ⁵⁄₁₆″ diameter 3.50

☐ Floral with painted rosebud, blue enamel border, ¼″ diameter 1.75

☐ Floral design in white enamel with black enamel background, convex, 1¹⁄₁₆″ diameter 1.50

☐ Fox chase scene, painted on white enamel background, copper rims and back, 1⅜″ diameter 4.00

☐ Harp design in green enamel with white relief, steel-studded border, 1⅛″ diameter 5.50

☐ Heart design in cobalt enamel, champleve, brass border with steel and engraving, ⁹⁄₁₆″ diameter 5.00

	CURRENT PRICE
☐ Holly design in natural color enamels, white background, 1⅛" diameter	3.25
☐ Leaf design in green enamels, notched-rim brass disc, ⁹/₁₆" diameter	1.75
☐ Star design, painted in blue and gold enamels, champleve, ⁵/₁₆" diameter	2.25

GLASS

We have known how to make glass from very early times; however, the origins of glass-making are somewhat obscure. Through the centuries the glass-maker learned that by adding certain minerals to the silica, a wide range of colored glass could be produced. It has now been established that by the beginning of the nineteenth century, glass-makers were producing glass in all the known colors and in a variety of textures.

It is almost certain that buttons have been made of glass for a very long time. They have been made from almost every form and type of glass available. Unfortunately, exact dating of glass buttons is almost impossible, as forms, decorative touches and colors have carried over from generation to generation. To complicate the matter, the type of shanks and the method of attaching the shanks also overlapped.

Glass buttons were produced in greater quantity than any other type of buttons and therefore can be found more easily. Most glass buttons found today will date from the late 1800s into the 1900s and can be purchased at a nominal price. Any button collector would find many hours of entertainment sorting through these buttons.

It should be noted:

1. Jet refers to highly polished, glossy black glass. It is not true jet.
2. Black buttons have a duller surface.
3. Jewel buttons are faceted glass (paste), usually in a metal setting.

Carmel-colored glass with black and gold raised highlights.
Three inset steel facets, 7/16″ diameter, $ .45 each.

CURRENT
PRICE

FIGURAL

☐ Ball, cranberry, 3/8″ diameter 1.00
☐ Ball, dark blue-green, wire shank, 1/2″
   diameter .... .75
☐ Berry, clear, light-green, wire shank, 1/2″
   diameter .... .80
☐ Cube, clear, blue-green, wire shank, 3/8″ ×
   3/8″ .... .20
☐ Eye, green glass, wire shank, 5/8″ diameter ..... .30
☐ Scallop shell, various colors and sizes .... .20

CURRENT
PRICE

JET

- ☐ Faceted, circa 1890s, 1″ diameter 8.00
- ☐ Flower incised in gold, self-shank, ⁷/₈″ diameter .... .40
- ☐ Flower in detail, convex back, four-way metal shank, ⁷/₈″ .... .40
- ☐ Flower painted on jet, large self-shank, ¹¹/₁₆″ × ¹¹/₁₆″ 1.25
- ☐ Flower design in silver and black, 1⁵/₁₆″ 1.50
- ☐ Flower all-over design. .... .50
- ☐ Flowers in geometric pattern on jet with dull background, 1⁹/₁₆″ diameter 1.00
- ☐ Geometric design with silver luster, metal shank, 1¹/₈″ diameter 1.50
- ☐ Gilt arrows on jet, brass shank and plate, 1¹/₈″ × ⁹/₁₆″ 5.50
- ☐ Paisley design, self-shank, 1¹/₆″ diameter .... .40
- ☐ Paisley design, incised in gold, red and blue, self-shank, ¹¹/₁₆″ × ¹¹/₁₆″ 3.00
- ☐ Peacock feather in iridescent jet, self-shank, ⁷/₈″ diameter 1.75
- ☐ Star design, slightly raised on dull finish background, ⁷/₈″ diameter .... .50
- ☐ Star with six points in gold luster, ⁷/₈″ diameter 1.25
- ☐ Various bits of jet cemented to a base, openwork metal back, loop-shank, various sizes 1.50

JEWELS

- ☐ Emerald, clear ball, wire shank, ³/₄″ diameter . 1.00
- ☐ Emerald, faceted, wire shank, ¹/₂″ diameter 1.00
- ☐ Emerald in filigree setting, ³/₄″ diameter 2.00
- ☐ Emerald set in heavy brass filigree setting, wire shank, 1¹/₆″ diameter 18.00

Jet-faceted buttons on original card, $^{11}/_{16}$″ diameter, $9.00 per card.

	CURRENT PRICE
☐ Emerald set in tin background, brass collet, wire shank, $^9/_{16}$″ diameter	14.00
☐ Emerald set in tin background, wire shank, $1^1/_2$″ diameter	12.00
☐ Garnet set in tin background, brass border	14.00
☐ Green opaque jewel in gold stone, wire shank, $^3/_8$″ diameter	2.00
☐ Peridot faceted ball, wire shank, $^5/_{16}$″	1.50
☐ Red jewel with impressed star design, wire shank, $^3/_8$″ diameter	2.00

MULTI-COLORED PLAIN GLASS

☐ Brown glass center set in ornate brass border, 2″ diameter	6.50
☐ Frosted glass over foil, metal back and rim, 1″ diameter	2.00
☐ Opaque glass with contrasting color and foil, slightly convex, $^1/_2$″ diameter	1.50
☐ Opaque rainbow-colored convex glass, molded shank, $^5/_8$″ diameter	5.00

CURRENT
PRICE

☐ Swirl design in black, purple, red and gray,
brass shank, ⅞″ diameter 4.00

☐ Swirl-design in purple, cut-steel border, brass
trim, encased in plastic, 2″ diameter 7.00

☐ Swirl, slag glass, sew through, various sizes 75

☐ Twisted glass on preformed core, one-color
lacy, self-shank, ⅜″ diameter 40

☐ Twisted glass on preformed core, two-color
spiral, metal shank, ½″ diameter 60

☐ Twisted glass on preformed core, three-color
spiral, self-shank, ½″ diameter 60

☐ Twisted glass in two colors spiraled around
surface of ball button, ⅜″ diameter 45

PAINTED

☐ Cross in enamel, jewel-type setting, ⅜″
diameter 75

☐ Ewer in enamel, jewel-type setting, oval 75

☐ Floral design painted and fired on surface, ⅝″
diameter 30

☐ Lilies and leaves in enamel, jewel-type setting,
¾″ diameter 75

☐ Mask, painted and fired over blue glass, 1⅛″
diameter 40

PRESSED

☐ Acorn and leaf design on black glass, ¾″
diameter 30

☐ Anchor design on opaque glass with silver lus-
ter, oval 1.00

☐ Animal design on iridescent black luster,
⅝″ diameter 3.00

☐ Balloon (hot air) design in high relief, steel
studded, ½″ diameter 3.50

☐ Bells (three) design with silver luster, ½″
diameter 1.25

☐ Bicycle design in low relief with silver luster,
1⅛″ diameter 1.25

☐ Building design, ⅝″ diameter 2.00

☐ Cameo head on black button 14.00

☐ Clover design of opaque glass with gold, silver
and polychrome touches, ⅝″ diameter 2.50

☐ Compass design on clambroth glass, 1″
diameter 1.50

☐ Cross design on opaque glass with luster trim,
¾″ diameter 1.75

☐ Cross design with milk glass center, embedded metal design, rimmed, tin back, 1″
diameter 8.00

☐ Cross design on mirror back, ¾″ diameter 2.25

☐ Crown design on black glass, luster touches,
1″ diameter 1.50

☐ Dice design on black glass, gold trim, ⅝″
diameter 1.75

☐ Elephant and palm tree design on black glass . 8.50

☐ Fan design on black glass, gilded, ¹¹/₁₆″
diameter 1.50

☐ Floral all-over design on brown glass, circa
1890s, 1″ diameter 2.50

☐ Floral basket design on black glass with iridescent luster, ¾″ diameter 1.75

☐ Floral basket design on transparent colored
glass, gilded, ornate trim, 1⅛″ diameter 1.50

☐ Floral design with colored decoration and sil-
ver luster, 1″ diameter 1.25

☐ Floral design on black glass, gold outline, ⅞″
diameter 1.60

Red glass pressed buttons with rose design highlighted in gold. Black painted rim, self-shank, ⅞" long, $ .45 each.

	CURRENT PRICE
☐ Floral design on opaque glass, ¾" diameter	2.00
☐ Geometric design on black glass filled with white pigment	.80
☐ Grape and leaves design on black glass, brass shank, pat. 1899, 1½" diameter	2.00
☐ House and windmill design on black glass, outlined with gold luster, self-shank, ¹¹⁄₁₆" diameter	2.25
☐ Knife, fork and spoon design on black glass, luster detail, ½" diameter	2.00
☐ Lacy design with gold luster touches, 1½" diameter	.50
☐ Lacy design with silver luster touches, ¾" diameter	.50
☐ Needlework design on black glass, various sizes	.40

UNDER GLASS (See Buttons, Paperweight)

☐ Black paint and gold leaf work on pearl, metal border, copper rim, tin back, 1½"	6.00
☐ Clear glass dome on tin with colored foil between, "Kaleidoscope," ⅝"	.50

Crystal, raised rim, square base, faceted underside, $^{15}/_{16}$" diameter, $ .85.

	CURRENT PRICE
☐ Feather, gilt rim, tin back	1.50
☐ Reverse painting on glass, deep blue background with metallic color trim, $1\frac{1}{2}$" diameter	4.00
☐ Star pattern of seed pearls on green background, convex lens, ivory back, copper shank, gilt rim, $1\frac{1}{2}$" diameter	18.00
☐ Watch crystal with pitch back, wire loop shank, $^{5}/_{8}$" diameter	3.00

HORN

Horn buttons have probably been made for a very long time. Their history is obscure, but by around 1760 it is believed that the first horn buttons were being made in America. Horn had been in use for some time, for it had been known that when it was subjected to long periods of heat it turned into maleable material. The horns as well as the hoofs from any domestic or wild animals could be used. They were simply placed in water, a mild solution of alkali or oil, and boiled for a few days. When the material was pliable, it could then be rolled open and placed between metal sheets for flattening. When cooled, it could be cleaned and scraped smooth. The finished product was then polished to a high shine. Most of the early horn buttons were plain; only a few have been known to be carved. However, since many different types of horns and hoofs were used, there can be a very interesting variation in the color of the buttons.

During the beginning of the nineteenth century another method of processing horns was introduced. The horns and hoofs were still boiled in the same manner, but the finished material was poured into hand molds in which they could be cooled and then removed. Interestingly, it is for this reason that horn has been called the early forerunner to plastic. This advanced technology proved to be quite a treat, because the hand molds, and later the machine molds, lent themselves quite nicely to the pressed picture buttons and more decorated horn buttons.

Horn buttons are listed alphabetically by the type of decoration.

CURRENT
PRICE

ABALONE

☐ Snowflake design inlay on horn button, 1″
diameter 1.75

METAL

☐ Crown design mounted on horn button, white
metal, 1¼″ diameter 1.00
☐ Floral design embedded on horn button, sew
through, ¾″ diameter 1.00
☐ Star design embedded on horn button, ⅝″
diameter .... .75

PAINTED

☐ Floral design in blue and white enamel, gilt in-
lays, ⁷⁄₁₆″ × ¹⁵⁄₁₆″ 1.60

PEARL

☐ Copper disk with carved pearl rim in center of
horn button, center fastened to shank, 1⅜″
diameter 2.00

CURRENT
PRICE

☐ Flowers in basket with metal inlay, ivory rim,
1⅛″ diameter, pressed horn 3.50
☐ Flowers (four), with gilt inlays, vertical hold,
¹⁵/₁₆″ diameter, pressed horn 2.25
☐ Leaf design on black horn button, 1½″
diameter 1.75
☐ Leaf design in horn button, 1⁵/₁₆″ diameter 1.60
☐ Painted wood and pearl square inlays on horn
button, ½″ diameter 1.50
☐ Star inlaid on light pressed horn, ⅝″
diameter 2.00
☐ Urn with flower inlay on pressed horn, ¹¹/₁₆″
diameter 2.45

PICTURE

☐ Acorn and leaf design on pressed horn, satin   1.25–
and matte finish, 1⅛″ 1.50
☐ Arrows in shape of cross on pressed horn, ⅞″   1.25–
× ⅞″ 1.50
☐ Balloon (hot air) design on pressed horn,   1.25–
black, ⅞″ diameter 1.50
☐ Bicycle design on pressed horn, dyed, various 1.25–
sizes 1.50
☐ Boot with spur in relief design on pressed   1.25–
horn, dyed, sew-through, ⅞″ diameter 1.50
☐ Butterfly design inlaid with silver and pearl on
pressed horn, ¾″ square 4.00
☐ Compass and square design on pressed horn,   1.25–
Masonic emblem, sew-through, ½″ diameter .. 1.50
☐ Corkscrew design on dyed black horn, sew   1.25–
through, ⅞″ diameter 1.50
☐ Dragonfly design in pearl and silver, pressed
horn, ⅝″ diameter 4.00
☐ Feather design on pressed horn, pin through   1.25–
center, ⅝″ diameter 1.50

CURRENT
PRICE

☐ Fleur-de-lis design in relief on pressed black horn, 1⅜″ diameter 1.25–1.50

☐ Floral center design inlaid with gilt, light metal and pearl on pressed horn, vertical hole, 1″ diameter 2.75

☐ Floral design on pressed horn, dyed, sew through, ¹¹⁄₁₆″ 1.00–1.25

☐ Floral design in relief on lined, convex ground, radiate from center on pressed horn, vertical hole, 1¹⁄₁₆″ 1.25–1.50

☐ Floral design in striped pattern on pressed horn, self-shank, 1³⁄₁₆″ 1.25–1.50

☐ Gun design on pressed horn, two-hole sew through, 1″ diameter 1.25–1.50

☐ Horseshoe design with white metal inlay on pressed horn, ¾″ diameter 1.60

☐ Lyre design on pressed black horn, ¾″ diameter 1.25–1.50

☐ Mythological heads in relief on pressed black horn, metal shank, 1¼″ 1.85

☐ Shells, conch, snail and scallop design in relief on pressed horn, 1″ diameter 1.25–1.50

☐ Train design in relief on black pressed horn, satin finish, lined background, 1⅛″ diameter 1.25–1.50

☐ Wheat design on pressed horn, sew through, various sizes 1.25–1.50

PLAIN

☐ Natural horn, cross-section, ⅞″ diameter .... .45–.55
☐ Natural horn, metal shank, ½″ diameter .... .45–.55
☐ Natural horn, sew through, ⁹⁄₁₆″ diameter .... .45–.55
☐ Natural horn tip, split lengthwise, ⅞″ × ⅞″ diameter 1.00–1.25
☐ Pressed horn, painted, sew through, various colors and sizes .... .45–.55

☐ Pressed horn to simulate textile patterns, var-
  ious sizes .... .45–.55
☐ Pressed horn to simulate tortoise shell, var-
  ious sizes 1.25

IVORY

Ivory buttons have been made for many centuries, mostly in Japan, China and Italy. Flowers, Oriental scenes and dragons were the most popular decorations on the Oriental ivory buttons, while flowers and birds were mostly featured on the Italian ivory buttons. Ivory buttons remained very popular from the 1860s until the turn of the century, when their popularity began to wane.

Ivory is a tough and translucent material that has a grain which is apparent under a magnifying glass. Old ivory should have a very soft tone. Any collector should be aware that materials that are relatively inexpensive are often used to make imitations of ivory. Sometimes ivory was used in combination with other materials as decorative touches or inlays. Also, always be on the lookout for ivory buttons made of walrus tusks; these are the rarest and are a collector's delight.

Ivory buttons are listed alphabetically by type of decoration.

CARVED

☐ Flowers carved in high relief, self-shank, 1⅛″
  diameter 25.00
☐ Stylized bird, ¾″ square, modern 8.00

ENAMEL

☐ Champleve butterflies on ivory disc, ¾″
diameter 32.00

FACETS, STEEL

☐ Concentric circles of ivory with facets set between, metal back, copper rim, 1⅛″
diameter 2.75
☐ Steel mirrors and facets set in ivory disc,
metal shank, 1″ diameter 4.50

PAINTED

☐ Basket painted on ivory under glass, gilt
chased rim, 1⅛″ diameter 5.50
☐ Bells painted in sepia on ivory under glass, silver mounting, 1⅛″ diameter 5.50
☐ Clock painted in sepia on ivory under glass,
silver rim, 1″ diameter 5.50
☐ Eye painted in sepia on ivory under glass, sil-
ver rim, 1″ diameter 5.50
☐ Eye painted in sepia on ivory under glass,
marcasites set in silver metal rim, ⅞″
diameter 8.50

LEATHER

Little is known about the origin of the leather button. However, it is certainly possible that craftsmen who worked in
leather to produce other objects would use the scraps to make
buttons. Old leather buttons are certainly not common, but
they were surely made. Our thrifty ancestors would not have
wasted usable bits of leather.

Most leather buttons were made by the same process
used to make cloth-covered buttons. The plain or decorated

leather was placed over a metal back which had an attached metal shank. Metal collets or metal rims were also used, but not as frequently. Decorative touches were added by tooling, embossing, and die stamping.

Leather buttons made today are usually very plain. If these buttons do have designs, they are usually very simple patterns of interwoven thin strips.

Leather buttons are listed alphabetically by the type of decoration.

CURRENT
PRICE

BRASS

☐ Key escutcheon, thick disc, ¾″ diameter 25

PLAIN

☐ Chamois over flat disc, 1½″ diameter 40
☐ Stitched rim, 1⅛″ diameter 45

PRESSED

☐ Leaf design, thick disc, ⅞″ diameter 30
☐ Leaf design with painted detail, metal shank,
    various sizes 35

TOOLED

☐ Star design, metal rim, 1¼″ diameter 75
☐ Sun design, metal rim, 1½″ diameter 80

WOVEN

☐ Strips, self-shank, 1½″ diameter, common 30

METAL

Buttons have long been made of many different metals. Gold and silver have been used, as well as the more common

Top left. Dark blue metal-stamped floral design in jewels, 1¼" diameter, $1.65. *Top right.* Open work floral design, ⅝" diameter, $ .85. *Middle right.* Stamped raised antique design, mottled background, metal shank, ¾" diameter, $ .60. *Bottom left.* Celluloid inset with steel facets in metal beaded rim, 1½" diameter, $3.00. *Bottom right.* Black metal background with raised white metal floral design, ⅝" diameter, $ .55.

metals such as brass, steel, aluminum, copper, pewter, pinchbeck, tin, German silver, and pot metals. Gold and sterling or solid silver buttons are very rare. In the early centuries such buttons were reserved for the nobility. It is interesting to note that they were often melted down to be reformed and redesigned.

The common person made do with buttons of other metals. Over the centuries metal buttons have been made in a variety of shapes and designs. With the commercial manufacture of metal buttons, a diverse number of designs were stamped and are still being made. Metal buttons are quite common in the market today and can be purchased for a nominal price.

Silver, pewter, steel and brass buttons are listed in separate categories.

Metal buttons are listed alphabetically by type of design.

☐ Airplane (early), stamped design, one-piece,
⁷/₈″ diameter .... .40–.50

☐ Anchor stamped design, self-shank, ⁵/₈″
diameter .... .40–.50

☐ Anchor stamped design, tinted, self-shank,
one-piece, various sizes .... .40–.50

☐ Anchor pierced and stamped design, tinted,
two-piece, various sizes .... .40–.50

☐ Anchor stamped design, studded with paste,
⁵/₈″ diameter .... .60–.70

☐ Anvil and hammer pierced and stamped de-
sign, tinted, one-piece, various sizes .... .40–.50

☐ Arrow stamped design, tinted, one-piece, ¹/₂″
diameter .... .40–.50

☐ Ax stamped design, tinted, two-piece, ¹/₂″
diameter .... .40–.50

☐ Balloon, hot air, stamped design, one-piece,
concave, cut steel trim, various sizes .... .40–.50

☐ Bamboo stamped design, bronze finish, var-
ious sizes .... .40–.50

☐ Beehive stamped design, tinted, two-piece,
1¹/₄″ diameter .... .60–.70

☐ Bicycle (high wheeler) stamped design in
white and yellow metal, various sizes .... .40–.50

☐ Bicycle (''Safety'') in relief on stamped metal
background, two-piece, various sizes .... .40–.50

☐ Boating scene stamped in relief on white and
yellow metal, two-piece, 1″ diameter 1.50

☐ Book stamped design, two-piece, ¹/₂″
diameter .... .40–.50

☐ Cactus stamped design, one-piece, 1¹/₁₆″ diam-
eter, copper 1.00

☐ Car on country road scene stamped on white
metal, tinted, two-piece, 1″ diameter .... .75

☐ Child's face in unfolding flower stamped design, brass border, ⁷/₈″ diameter 1.25

	CURRENT PRICE
☐ Crown stamped design in relief on white and yellow metal, two-piece, ⅝″ diameter	1.00
☐ Cupid and robin stamped design, tin back, 1⅙″ diameter	.70
☐ Cupid and torch stamped design, tin back, ¾″ diameter	2.50
☐ Dice set on face with pierced white metal cube, ⅝″ diameter	2.00
☐ Dragon and moon stamped design on painted background, tin, 1¹⁄₁₆″ diameter	1.50
☐ Eagle head stamped design, one-piece, ¾″ diameter	3.00
☐ Elizabeth II stamped design, 2¼″ diameter	15.00
☐ Fan stamped design on white and yellow metal, two-piece, 1⅛″ diameter	1.00
☐ Floral stamped design on various metals mounted on various backs, tinted, various sizes	.40–.50
☐ Floral stamped design in relief, matte surface, gilt touches, 1¼″ diameter	.60
☐ Floral stamped design in relief, pebbled background, one-piece, 1″ diameter	.75
☐ Floral stamped design in interlocking pattern, concave, tin back, 1⅙″ diameter	.70
☐ Floral stamped design with cut-out background, set glass jewel in center, 1¾″ diameter	1.50
☐ Floral stamped design, aluminum, 1½″ diameter	2.00
☐ Girl at gate stamped design, amethyst tint, ½″ diameter	4.00
☐ Lyre stamped design, steel-studded, ⅝″ diameter	.80
☐ Mask stamped design on white and yellow metal, one-piece, 1½″ diameter	1.00
☐ Pagoda stamped design, recessed center, tinted, tin, 1″ diameter	1.25

	CURRENT PRICE
☐ Portrait on tin, brass rim, ½″	5.00
☐ Pyramids and buildings stencil design, painted tin set in metal, 1″ diameter	2.00
☐ Rose, thistle and shamrock stamped design, tin, 1″ diameter	.85
☐ Shield-shaped, yellow and white metal, one-piece	.80
☐ Ship and figures, stamped design, tinted, tin, various sizes	.85
☐ Simulated cut steel stamped on white metal, tinted in various colors and sizes	.40–.50
☐ Swan stamped design, gilt, convex, ⅞″ diameter	1.50
☐ Viking profile stamped design, black background, brass and nickel, ¹⁵⁄₁₆″ diameter	2.00
☐ Wheat stamped and pierced design, tinted, two-piece, various sizes	.40–.50

PAPERWEIGHT

Paperweight buttons first made their appearance during the middle of the 1800s. They exhibit a delicate and highly skilled craftsmanship. To be classified as a paperweight, the button must have a separate center design with layers of glass fused over it. Many designs can be found in paperweight buttons, but flowers are certainly a favorite.

Paperweight buttons as a classification are certainly the most expensive buttons to be found. Shank plates with a wire loop shank, as well as the four-way shank, are found only on newer paperweight buttons.

	CURRENT PRICE
☐ Blue flower with green leaves	12.00
☐ Cane in small embedded pieces, heavy shank	16.00

☐ Canes, two-colored in spirals, low convex,
　½″ diameter 18.00
☐ Canes, two-colored in swirls, low convex, ⅝″
　diameter 19.00
☐ Chrysanthemum, white with yellow center 18.00
☐ Colored glass dab fused over metal shank,
　color reflects, ⅝″ diameter 8.00
☐ Daisy with green leaves 15.00
☐ Foil design, frosted glass covering 6.00
☐ Millville Rose 28.00
☐ Random design of goldstone and dark flecks,
　crystal glass 10.00
☐ Red rose, ¾″ diameter 20.00
☐ Pink flower with green center, ½″ diameter 22.00
☐ Spiral ribbon, ⁹⁄₁₆″ diameter 15.00

PEARL

Pearl buttons are made from ocean and fresh water shells.
The process of turning shells into buttons is long, involves
many steps, and takes skillful craftsmanship. During the
eighteenth century, pearl buttons were hand-made and
scarce. Pearl buttons began to appear in much greater quantity about 1850 when mass production became feasible. But
even with power-driven tools, the process of turning out a
finished button is a long one.

The beautiful iridescence of the shell itself makes a plain,
undecorated button look lovely. Many collectors prefer the
unadorned button. However, pearl buttons were quite often
carved, engraved, painted and used in combination with
other materials for decoration. Pearl buttons have also been
made in many sizes. They have been made as sew-through
buttons and with metal shanks. Interesting to note is that
today some so-called pearl buttons are really made from a

Top left. Round pearl button with raised middle ring, $7/16''$ diameter, $1.50. *Top right.* One-piece pearl button with raised middle oval ring, $11/16''$ diameter, $1.50. *Bottom left.* Convex smoky pearl in a shallow brass rim, metal shank, $1.25. *Bottom right.* Smoky pearl, one-piece raised round center, metal shank, $2.50.

powdered substance that is reconstituted and mechanically turned into buttons.

Pearl buttons are listed alphabetically by the type of decoration.

CURRENT
PRICE

ABALONE

☐ Ovals inlaid on white pearl base,
 $1\frac{1}{4}''$ diameter 5.00

BRASS

☐ Art Nouveau swirl lines on white disc,
 $1''$ diameter 4.00
☐ Filigree brass base and border with encased
 pearl, $1\frac{1}{8}''$ diameter 2.50
☐ Pearl base with brass stamped basket of flow-
 ers, metal frame, $7/8''$ diameter 1.75
☐ Plain brass base with encased engraved pearl,
 $1''$ diameter 2.25

BRONZE

☐ Pearl base with bronze and bead grapes,
$^{15}/_{16}$″ diameter 6.00

CARVED

☐ Bird on plain base, $^3/_4$″ diameter 1.00
☐ Crane, sew through, $^5/_8$″ 1.00
☐ Fan design in relief, metal rim and back,
$1^1/_2$″ diameter 6.00
☐ Floral design, metal shank, $^7/_{16}$″ diameter 1.50
☐ Grillwork center, plain edge, brass shank,
$1^3/_4$″ diameter 4.00
☐ Pierced and carved set over foil, gilt rim,
$1^1/_2$″ diameter 2.50
☐ Rose, $^1/_2$″ diameter .... .75
☐ Snowflake in graded relief, $1^1/_8$″ diameter 4.25
☐ Steel-studded rim, carved pearl center, metal
shank, 1″ diameter 3.00

ENGRAVED

☐ Floral design with metal pin through center to
make shank, 1″ diameter 2.50
☐ Floral design on convex pearl, vertical hole,
$1^1/_6$″ diameter 2.50
☐ Floral design on smoky pearl, four-hole sew
through, $1^1/_2$″ diameter 2.00
☐ Snowflake design on dark green pearl, 1″
diameter 1.25
☐ Star, pierced design with engraved detail, 1″
diameter 5.50

FIGURAL

☐ Cat's eye, sometimes colored, metal shank,
various sizes .... .40–.50

Carved iridescent pearl, ¹⁵/₁₆″ diameter, $1.95 each.

	CURRENT PRICE
☐ Duck with grooved detail, ⅝″ long	1.00
☐ Fan, smoky pearl, two-hole sew through	1.25
☐ Flower, metal shank, ⅞″ diameter	1.00
☐ Flower, sew through, ⅞″ diameter	1.00
☐ New moon (crescent), smoky pearl, ⅝″ long ...	1.25

PLAIN

☐ Imitation four-hole sew through, brass shank, 1⅙″ diameter	2.00
☐ Round, dyed blue, 1″ diameter	.25
☐ Round, metal shank, on original card of six, ¼″ diameter	4.00
☐ Round, two-hole sew through, very large holes	.50
☐ Round, two-hole sew through, on original card of six, ⅝″ diameter	3.50
☐ Smoky pearl, oval, 1⅝″ long	1.25
☐ Vertical hole	.35

SMOKY PEARL

☐ Engraved center inlay on white pearl base, 1″
diameter 4.00
☐ Diamond shapes inlaid on white pearl base,
1¼″ diameter 4.00
☐ Discs in chased aluminum mounts set in
white pearl base, ⅞″ diameter 4.50

STEEL

☐ Tinted green pearl with steel escutcheon, 1″
diameter 2.50
☐ Three-faceted stones set in white disk 1.35

PEWTER

Pewter buttons have been made since the fifteenth century. The properties of pewter have always made it an excellent, if not particularly durable, material to use. Since it melts at low temperatures, people with a mold could make pewter buttons at home. For example, in America, household utensils, when totally worn out, were often melted down and made into buttons.

A few early pewter buttons were stamped out of flat sheets of pewter and then decorated in simple designs with a die stamp. These buttons were usually flat and had a soldered eye shank. However, most pewter buttons were made in a mold. If they were to have a particular design, it was incorporated into that mold. With the help of a die-stamped steel punch, a few were initialled or decorated with an insignia after being removed from the mold.

Pewter buttons are listed alphabetically by the design.

☐ Calla lily design in high relief, concave dark
green background, ⅞″ diameter 1.50

☐ Cupid and drum design, tin background, wire
shank, ¹¹/₁₆″ diameter 2.50

☐ Daisy design with pearl flower head, bright
cut trim, ⅝″ diameter 1.50

☐ Daisy over Greek key arch, flat, stippled background, 1″ diameter 1.25

☐ Escutcheon and geometric design on brass
disc, ½″ diameter .... .30

☐ Fan design stamped and pierced, fan of white
metal, pewter back, 1″ diameter 2.75

☐ Geometric stamped and pierced design, 1″
diameter 1.25

☐ Leaf stamped design, 1″ diameter .... .75

☐ Little girl in wreath design, steel back, one-
piece, wire shank, ⁹/₁₆″ diameter 2.00

☐ New moon stamped design, tinted, backmark
"T," ⅝″ diameter 1.50

☐ Owl's head design 5.50

☐ Star stamped and pierced design, ⅝″
diameter .... .40

☐ Star design, die-struck, various sizes .... .40

☐ Ugly duckling, swan and bulrush design,
hand-painted, 1½″ diameter 8.00

☐ Victorian girl with parasol design in high re-
lief, brass back, ⅝″ 4.00

☐ Windmill, tree and house scene stamped in
pewter, 1″ diameter 1.75

SILVER

Solid silver, continental silver and hallmarked silver buttons
were undoubtedly made, but are very rarely found in today's

market. The silver buttons that the collector would most likely find, are silver-plated buttons. These were commercially manufactured in the late 1800s and 1900s and designs were always stamped.

Silver buttons are listed alphabetically by the type of decoration. It can be assumed that they are all silver-plated unless otherwise noted.

CURRENT
PRICE

ENGRAVED

☐ Cherub heads with rope design border, hall-
marked, 1″ diameter 24.00
☐ Egyptian woman's head, sterling 21.00
☐ Indian head in relief, ⅝″ diameter 8.00
☐ Thailand design, niello, circa 1940, ½″
diameter 8.50

FILIGREE

☐ Silver filigree and fine wire decoration, shot
work, set in enamel and stones 12.00

JEWEL

☐ Geometric design button set with turquoise,
copper shank, ¹⁵/₁₆″ diameter 4.00

PICTURE, STAMPED

☐ Anchor stamped design in relief, sterling silver
border, ½″ diameter 14.00
☐ Automobile stamped design in relief, 1¼″
diameter 2.00
☐ Fat boy stamped design on concave silvered
background, one-piece, wire shank, ¹¹/₁₆″
diameter 3.00
☐ Clover leaf design, one-piece, sterling silver 8.00

☐ Clovers and flowers, cut-out background, 1⅜″
diameter 3.50
☐ Crane and cattails design on silver-plated
brass, tin back, wire shank, ¾″ diameter 2.00
☐ Floral design on silver-plated pierced back-
ground, 1″ diameter 7.00
☐ Floral design, ¹¹/₁₆″ diameter 1.50
☐ Little Fish and the Fisherman, 1⅛″
diameter 38.00
☐ Mask with surrounding design stamped on
one-piece button, 1″ diameter 8.00
☐ Men drinking design stamped on one-piece
button, ¹⁵/₁₆″ diameter 7.50
☐ Rose design stamped on ball-shaped button,
self-shank, 1⅛″ diameter 1.00
☐ Sailing ship design stamped on disc, inset in
steel button, ¾″ diameter 5.00
☐ Wounded stag design, two-piece, wire shank,
¹¹/₁₆″ diameter 3.00

STEEL

Matthew Boulton first delighted Birmingham, England, with
cut steel buttons during the middle of the eighteenth century. These buttons were actually an imitation of a reproduction. That is, they were made to look like marcasite, which
was made to reproduce the shape of a diamond. During this
process, individually cut facets were riveted to place on a
solid piece of metal. Pieces could be made of more than one
hundred individual facets of steel. However, riveted buttons
were seldom made after the first quarter of the nineteenth
century because about that time a much quicker and easier
method was devised. Now, a pattern could simply be stamped
onto a piece of steel. Both types were decorated by gilding,
plating and decorating with pearls or stones. Later, steel

buttons were often tinted, and by the late nineteenth century they were being used to decorate buttons of velvet, bone, silk, rubber, horn, glass, wood, shell, brass, vegetable ivory and other materials.

Steel buttons are listed alphabetically by type of decoration.

CURRENT
PRICE

BRASS

☐ Lyre superimposed on steel back, steel rim, ⅝″ diameter .... .85
☐ Round blue iridescent bowl shape steel, brass filigree back, ¾″ diameter 5.50

ETCHED

☐ Floral design, 1″ diameter 4.75
☐ Floral design on dark tinted background, 1″ diameter 5.50
☐ Floral design, set in recessed steel back, steel rim, 1⅜″ diameter 5.75

FACETS

☐ All-over design, individually riveted to concave brass base, 1¼″ diameter 2.90
☐ All-over design, stamped and applied to brass back, ⅞″ diameter .... .75
☐ Blue iridescent center and facets individually riveted to brass back, filigree border 4.50
☐ Bow with facets in white metal recessed background, ⅞″ diameter 2.75
☐ Cluster, 100 individually riveted to brass back, circa 1890, 1⅛″ diameter 3.00
☐ Cluster, 50 individually riveted to white metal back, circa 1890, ⅞″ diameter 2.00
☐ Cluster, individually riveted to scalloped brass base, ⁵⁄₁₆″ diameter .... .90

☐ Cluster, individually riveted to brass, center in cameo-carved pearl, ⅞″ diameter 8.65

☐ Dome-shape center and facets individually riveted to aluminum back and border, ½″ diameter 1.40

☐ Geometric design, individually riveted to brass base, 1½″ diameter 3.75

☐ Moon design (crescent) and three stars design, individually riveted to brass base, brass border finely detailed roses, ¾″ diameter 1.60

☐ One-steel, riveted on pierced brass and steel back, various sizes 50

☐ Spoke design, individually riveted in center of brass disc, ⅝″ diameter 75

PEARL

☐ Carved and pierced pearl, solid steel back and trim, steel shank, 1″ diameter 1.25

☐ Round pearls and steel facets mounted over green velvet, steel back, cut steel rim, 1¼″ diameter 2.50

STAMPED

☐ Floral design, four-sided in relief, pebbled background, one-piece, 1³⁄₁₆″ diameter 1.85

☐ Floral design in relief, one-piece, 1″ diameter 1.50

☐ Leaf design, tinted, matte background, gilded, 1″ diameter 1.35

☐ Star design in relief, ¾″ diameter 1.25

☐ Star design in relief, tinted, ¾″ diameter 1.25

VEGETABLE IVORY

Vegetable ivory is made from the Corozo nut of the palms that grow in parts of Central and South America. It was first introduced to Europe in 1862 and shortly thereafter to America. Vegetable ivory became a favorite material for the manufacture of buttons because it was inexpensive, durable, could be easily worked and could be dyed and stained. However, it does not appear in a great variety of colors because vegetable ivory could only be stained on the surface. Unfortunately, a stained button of vegetable ivory with drilled holes appears white under the surface. Vegetable ivory buttons can be found with self-shanks, brass shanks and as two- and four-hole sew-through buttons.

Vegetable ivory buttons are listed alphabetically by the type of decoration.

	CURRENT PRICE
☐ Axes crossed impressed design, self-shank, ½″ diameter	.35–.45
☐ Door knocker impressed design, painted ring superimposed, self-shank	.35–.45
☐ Fleur-de-lis impressed design, satin black finish disc, ⅞″ diameter	.50
☐ Floral impressed design, dyed in solid color, various sizes	.35–.45
☐ Geometric impressed design, dyed in solid color, highly polished, ¾″ diameter	.35–.45
☐ Greek key impressed design, brown, ⅞″ diameter	.35–.45
☐ Grid impressed design, black background, 1⅛″ diameter	.30
☐ Head, helmeted with plumes, impressed design, self-shank, ⅝″ diameter	.75
☐ Horseshoe and riding crop, impressed design, self-shank, ⅝″ diameter	.75
☐ Man on a horse, impressed design, ⅞″ diameter	.75

☐ Moon cut-out design on painted plaid finish
background, brown and black, ³/₄″ diameter ...   1.00
☐ Star impressed design, light brown, 1″
diameter 35–.45
☐ Star carved and pierced design, ½″ diameter ..   1.50

WOOD

Wood buttons have probably been made for many centuries, as wood has always been accessible to most people. Early wood buttons are found in simple undecorated forms. However, these can be quite beautiful as the wood is usually cut diagonally and shows the natural grain. During the 1800s wood buttons were carved, painted and combined with other materials to add decorative touches. By the late 1800s wood picture buttons appeared. These buttons had a very shallow pressed design and were often elaborate. They were strictly of a commercial quality and the majority of wood buttons found in the market today come from this period and later. Although these types of buttons are somewhat easier to date, the same is not true of the plain wood button with sew-through holes. Because they have always been made in essentially the same way, they would be very difficult to date.

CARVED

☐ Teakwood in floral pattern, late 75
☐ Teakwood in geometric pattern, late 75

PLAIN

☐ Brass rim with wood center, 1¼″ diameter 50
☐ Colored, laminated, sew-through, any size 25
☐ Contrasting colors, laminated, metal shank 25

Diagonally sliced plain wood buttons. Leather band, 1¼″ long, $ .50 each.

	CURRENT PRICE
☐ Pearl insert in wood base, ¾″ diameter	1.25
☐ Plastic trim on wood base, sew through, 1³/₁₆″ diameter	.35
☐ Steel disc on wood base, 1″ diameter	.75

PRESSED

☐ Floral design on high convex button, metal shank, 1″ diameter	.85

Left. Natural wood, ⅝″ diameter, $ .20. *Right.* Pressed wood button with painted detail, yellow, blue, red and pink flowers with green leaves, ⁹/₁₆″ diameter, $ .40.

CURRENT
PRICE

☐ Floral design on pierced teakwood, self-shank,
1¼″ diameter 1.00
☐ Ocean liner, painted, sew through .... .40
☐ Skier, painted, sew through, any size .... .40

Catalogs
and Booklets

Old catalogs and booklets can be a wonderful source of information and enjoyment for the collector. First, they can help date items as well as fashions. However, their beauty is not only in the time frame which they give us, but in their capacity to provide details on items that might have otherwise gone unnoticed. For example, we have learned about trims, bindings, zippers, and all sorts of sewing accessories. We have gathered information and amusing anecdotes on sizes, materials and colors of particular items and the fashions they inspired.

Booklets are a great source of old sewing and needlework patterns. They often include detailed instructions on needlework methods, fashion design, and the use of accessories in fashion.

General catalogs of the past can be just plain enjoyable reading. It is fascinating to see what was being worn or used in the past. It is also fun to see how prices have changed. The

Published by Woman's Institute of Domestic Arts & Sciences, Inc., Scranton, PA. *Left.* 1925 Ribbon and Fabric Trimmings, $12.00. *Right.* 1916 Embroidery and Decorative Stitches, $15.00.

price of a thimble as it appears in the 1902 *Sears, Roebuck Catalog* is indeed very interesting. Thimbles made of aluminum were listed at $ .08 per dozen. If you preferred, you could buy a German silver or gilt one for $ .03 each. A silver-plated thimble cost $ .04 each. Sterling silver embossed embroidery scissors were listed at $ .95.

Catalogs and booklets are easy to find at a nominal price. They abound at flea markets and shows, especially Paper Collectibles shows. As with all paper collectibles, catalogs and booklets should be in very good condition. This means they should be clean, with no tears, bends or creases.

Catalogs and booklets are listed alphabetically by the company.

The Sears, Roebuck Catalog, 1902 reprint edition, $5.00.

	CURRENT PRICE
☐ Alden's, Spring & Summer, 1954, Chicago, mail order catalog (fashions)	10.00
☐ Butterick Dressmaker	14.00
☐ Butterick Dressmaking, 1927, salesman's sample	40.00
☐ Crochetcraft, 1910	20.00
☐ Davis Sewing Machine, 1874, 40 pages	12.00
☐ Delineator, "Paris Frocks at Home," circa 1930	24.00
☐ Dietzgen Measuring Tapes, 1920, 24 pages	8.50
☐ Doilies to Treasure	10.00
☐ Domestic Sewing Machine with Palmer Cox Brownies	8.00
☐ How to Crochet Cluny Lace, booklet	10.00

CURRENT
PRICE

☐ McCall, Complete Catalog of McCall Design,
1933 .... 20.00

☐ Mexican Drawn Work, 50 Designs, booklet,
1898 .... 10.00

☐ Montgomery Ward Fall and Winter Catalog,
1928 .... 35.00

☐ Montgomery Ward Spring and Summer Cata-
log, 1935 .... 35.00

☐ Montgomery Ward Fall and Winter Catalog 12.50

☐ Montgomery Ward Winter Catalog, 1953 .... 5.00

☐ Montgomery Ward Sewing Machines, early
1900s 40.00

☐ Sears, Roebuck Fall and Winter Catalog, 1935 24.00

☐ Sears, Roebuck Spring and Summer Catalog,
1955 .... 5.00

☐ Sears Christmas Catalog, 1960 .... 5.00

☐ Sears, Roebuck Catalog, 1902 reprint edition,
Crown Publishers, 1969 .... 5.00

☐ Singer Sewing Machine Co. Catalog, 1900, 30
pages 15.00

☐ Singer Sewing Machine Co. Catalog, 1908, 32
pages 24.00

☐ Singer Sewing Machine Co. Catalog, 1920 ...... 12.00

☐ Woman's Institute of Domestic Arts & Sciences, Inc., Scranton, PA, "Ribbon and Fabric
Trimmings," 1925, 45 pages 12.00

☐ Woman's Institute of Domestic Arts & Sciences, Inc., Scranton, PA, "Underwear and
Lingerie," 2 volumes, 1925 .... 18.00

Chatelaines

ॐ ॐ ॐ ॐ ॐ ॐ ॐ ॐ ॐ ॐ

A chatelaine is a collection of sewing, small household and personal objects hung from chains or cords. These are then attached to a ring or plaque (an ornamental brooch) which is fastened to a belt at the waist. The word "chatelaine" loosely translates to "mistress of the house" and the chatelaine was worn by women to keep all of these little items accessible. Many small items such as memo pads, picks, pencils, pin cushions, scent bottles, scissors and thimbles, were attached. In many ways the chatelaine could be considered to serve the same purpose as a purse.

Chatelaines have been in and out of fashion from at least the seventeenth century and have been made of many materials. Some of the more commonly found materials are gold, silver and other metals. Some chatelaines were very plain but many, particularly when made of silver and gold, were highly decorated with ivory, small jewels and mother-of-pearl. Chatelaines come in a broad price range; they can cost from $100 to thousands of dollars.

Chatelaines are listed alphabetically by the material of

which they are made. They are only listed if they have one
or more sewing or needlework implements attached. Price
guides to jewelry would list other chatelaines.

CURRENT
PRICE

GOLD-FILLED

☐ Shield plaque, single link chains connecting to
a pincushion and a memo pad, double link
chain connecting to a pencil, mother-of-pearl
inserts, circa 1880 .... 325.00

JET

☐ Heavy twisted jet plaque, faceted and polished
jet, five twisted jet cords connect to pencil
holder, memo pad, scissors with case, pin
cushion and thimble holder, circa 1865 .... 475.00

LEATHER

☐ Leather knot plaque, three thin leather straps
connect to scissors in case, thimble holder and
pencil, circa 1900, English 185.00
☐ Ring top connects to leather purse, thin
leather straps connect to memo pad and pencil, scissors with case, mirror and scent bottle,
circa 1900, English 385.00

PINCHBECK (Metal made of copper and zinc)

☐ Openwork pinchbeck, three-part plaque with
thimble case attached at bottom, circa 1780,
English 400.00
☐ Shield plaque, three braided pinchbeck chains
connect to two needle cases and scissors case,
circa 1790 .... 450.00

CURRENT
PRICE

SILK

☐ Plain ring top, red silk and ivory cords with
ivory rings connect to ivory bodkin, hole
maker, strawberry-shaped emery cushion,
needle, pin holder 95.00

STERLING SILVER

☐ Chased and embossed, sterling silver griffin
and snake plaque, three sterling chains connect to sliding mirror, scissors case and scent
bottle, circa 1890 .... 525.00
☐ Plain sterling silver ring top, sterling silver
chains connect to note pad with three ivory inserts, thimble and thimble case, needle holder,
nineteenth century 500.00
☐ Plain sterling silver ring top, sterling silver
chains connect to note pad with five ivory inserts, thimble and thimble case, buttonhook,
English 500.00
☐ Plain sterling silver ring top, five plain sterling
silver chains connect to round pin cushion,
memo pad with mother-of-pearl cover, pick,
pencil and square pin cushion, circa 1880 ...... 495.00
☐ Plain sterling silver ring top, three plain sterling silver chains connect to round pincush-
ion, pick and pencil 190.00
☐ Plain sterling silver ring top, two plain sterling
silver chains connect to etui (a small fitted
case to hold thimble, scissors, pick, etc.) and
notebook, hallmarked, circa 1880 .... 450.00
☐ Plain sterling silver ring top, five plain sterling
silver chains connect to scissors, thimble, tape
measure, pincushion, smelling salts 525.00
☐ Sterling silver heart plaque, sterling silver
double plain chain to thimble in case and single sterling silver chain to pencil, circa 1880 .. 340.00

CURRENT
PRICE

YELLOW METAL

☐ Lady's head plaque, three yellow metal open
work chains connect to memo pad, scissors
case, thimble case and pencil, circa 1870 ....   190.00
☐ Open work plaque, three open work chains
connect to pincushion, needle case and scis-
sors with case, circa 1870 ....   190.00

Crochet Tools

Crocheting is simply done by pulling one loop of thread through another loop. It is probably a type of needlework that has been done for centuries, for children have always enjoyed making designs by pulling loops through loops with their fingers. However, as a form of needlework, it was little known until the potato famine hit Ireland. At that time orders of Irish nuns started creating crochet lace in imitation of Venetian lace and the old Italian laces. These pieces were then sold to raise money to feed the poor and starving in Ireland. It was a laborious task, but certainly faster than making the hand-made laces of the time. This became known as Irish crochet or lace. Many women were taught this art and the lace became very fashionable and in demand. With the great exodus of the Irish people to America, the art of crochet was brought here. In America, the art of crocheting rapidly spread; women devised their own patterns and designs and it quickly became an American art form. American lace crochet is unique.

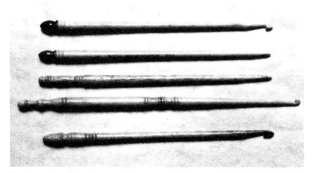

Crochet hooks. *Top to bottom.* Ivory, size 4, $11.00; ivory, size 5, $11.00; bone, $2.00; ivory, $12.00; bone, $4.00.

All that is needed to crochet is a hooked needle and some thread.

The crochet hook is held in one hand and the thread in the other. Working swiftly and with a variety of stitches and threads, beautiful patterns and designs can be created to produce a tremendous variety of original and very lovely items. It is not really known where these stitches or designs originated, but they have added beauty and originality to the history of American crochet.

Crochet work has produced wonderful patterns for coverlets, tablecloths, rugs, afghans, and articles of clothing, but the truly original and lovely American crochet has been concentrated in the laces.

Crochet hooks are listed alphabetically by the material of which they are made.

CURRENT
PRICE

BONE

☐ Finial end, circa 1915, 5″	2.50
☐ Handles, steel hook	3.50
☐ Plain, early	15.00
☐ With ivory, circa 1930, 4¼″	2.00

CURRENT
PRICE

CELLULOID

☐ Ivory color, 5½" 3.00

IVORY

☐ Carved 12.50
☐ Plain 11.00
☐ Two ivory punches and crochet hook in box ... 55.00

STEEL

☐ Two steel and one bone crochet hooks in
round wood case, circa 1900 .... 22.00

WHALE BONE

☐ Carved, set of three 225.00

Darning Balls
and Darning Eggs

As the name implies, darning balls and darning eggs were tools used to provide a firm foundation while darning stockings. Naturally, they were most commonly found to be round or egg-shaped, although other shapes such as mushroom, strawberry and bell have been made. It must be obvious that any hard material could have been used to darn stockings. Indeed, thrifty women of the past used their imagination and the items around them, even dried gourds. Women of the present day must have taken a lesson or two from their mothers, because they commonly make use of such modern-day inventions as the burned-out light bulb.

Unlike the darning balls we use today, early ones did not have handles. When handles were added, they were generally made of the same material as the ball or egg. The most common materials used to make darning balls were wood, glass, ivory and bone. It wasn't until the late nineteenth century and early twentieth century that the once plain handles

Ivory miniature darning egg, 1¼″, $12.00.

became elaborate, with decorations, and were often made of sterling silver. Sometimes, these handles had a practical side, but only if they could be unscrewed to provide a place for the darning needles and thread. Generally, darning balls are six to seven inches long if they have a handle. The ball alone is usually three to four inches in diameter.

Darning egg. Milk glass, 3″ long, $20.00.

Darning eggs. *Top.* Black painted wood, $6.00. *Bottom.* Natural painted wood, $6.00.

Darning balls and eggs are listed alphabetically by the material from which they are made.

CURRENT
PRICE

CELLULOID

☐ Ball, with metal handle 10.00
☐ Bell shape, with handle 8.00

GLASS

☐ Amber ball, blown, with amber knob
handle 40.00
☐ Aqua ball, blown 35.00
☐ Blue ball, blown, with white pulled loops
(Nailsea) 110.00
☐ Cased ball, blown, marbelized pattern 115.00
☐ Cobalt blue ball, blown, with ribbed handle 125.00
☐ Green ball, blown 45.00
☐ Peachblow ball, New England, shiny finish 225.00
☐ Red ball, pressed 25.00
☐ Red and gold ball, blown 35.00

Darning egg. Wood, flat base and rounded top, spring fits into groove to hold stocking, 1⁷/₈″ diameter, $2.50.

	CURRENT PRICE
☐ Ruby ball, blown, with handle	30.00
☐ Spatter ball, blown	95.00

IVORINE

☐ Plain, with baluster handle	20.00

WOOD

☐ Advertising, Banbury & Burnett, Inc., Fine Rug Cleaning, with handle	8.00
☐ Carved pattern handle	12.00
☐ Dark and light woods, Shaker	45.00
☐ Dark finish wood, with handle	7.00
☐ Dark finish wood, flat mushroom base	8.00
☐ Ebony, with plain ebony handle	15.00
☐ Ebony, with sterling silver embossed handle ...	40.00
☐ Ebony, with sterling silver plain handle	35.00
☐ Ebony, with sterling silver ornate embossed handle	45.00
☐ Hardwood, with carved pattern handle	12.00
☐ Hardwood, with turned handle, Shaker	45.00

Ebony egg. Sterling silver handle with raised floral and scroll decoration, 5¾" long, $45.00.

	CURRENT PRICE
☐ Maple, with removable needle case, Shaker	80.00
☐ Painted in oils of harbor scene	34.00
☐ Painted in marbleized pattern	28.00
☐ Painted, lacquered Oriental scenes	25.00
☐ Painted, with red and green stripes	12.00
☐ Walnut, mushroom shape, with handle	15.00
☐ Walnut, egg shape, with handle	15.00

WHALE BONE

| ☐ Plain, with wood handle, small .... | 80.00 |

Darning Sticks

A darning stick was a tool designed to facilitate the mending of gloves. It was designed with a handle in the middle to which different size knobs were attached to each end. They were approximately six inches to eight inches in length and easily slipped into the fingers of the glove to provide a firm foundation for the darning. Although most darning sticks were made entirely of wood, a few can be found with sterling silver handles. Although darning balls and eggs are still being made, the same is not true of the darning stick, since gloves no longer enjoy their once important status in high fashion.

CURRENT
PRICE

STERLING SILVER

☐ Plain handle, wood knobs 30.00

	CURRENT PRICE
☐ Plain handle, sterling silver knobs	45.00
☐ Repousse handle, plain sterling silver knobs ...	50.00

WOOD

☐ Plain wood handle, wood knobs	10.00

Embroidery Tools

❦❦❦❦❦❦❦❦❦❦

Embroidery is certainly the oldest form of needlework in existence. It is evident that from the beginning of history people have been fascinated with decorating themselves, their clothing and their homes. Embroidering offered a perfect medium for achieving this, because all the equipment that was needed to embroider was a needle, thread, fabric, and perhaps a hoop.

Embroidering is simply the application of threads, in patterns and designs, to fabric. There are a vast number of embroidery stitches that, when applied with threads of all types to a variety of fabrics, can produce countless effects. Embroidery can really be considered an art form. It is like painting on cloth. It is truly a medium for self-expression and provides hours of pleasure, joy and self-satisfaction for the needleworker.

For many centuries throughout Europe, embroidery was the art of the "Gentlewoman." The upper-class woman was expected to be very adept at needlework and spent much of her time so employed. Little girls were taught their stitches from an early age. Since travel was restricted, regional differences appear in embroidery. Different countries produced distinctive embroidery work and stitches.

In America, most women, at some time, embroidered. All of the women immigrating to this country brought with them their stitches and designs. These were passed from woman to woman, place to place, and by the eighteenth and nineteenth centuries a distinctive American style of embroidery was taking shape. Little girls in America were taught their stitches at home from a very early age. Embroidery and needlework were taught in "young ladies' " schools. Everyone is probably familiar with the embroidered samplers.

Crewel work, cross stitch, candlewicking, needlepoint, counted thread and many other types of needlework are really offshoots of embroidery. They employ the same stitches as embroidery but vary the thread or the material being worked.

Although it is not necessary, an embroidery hoop is a great help in embroidering. A hoop is a pair of rings with one

Wood, hand formed, 6″ oval, $7.00.

slightly smaller than the other. The fabric is placed over the smaller ring and the larger ring pushed down over both. This helps hold the fabric taut. Hoops come in various sizes. Hoops can be hand-held, be a part of a standing frame or be attached to a table clamp mechanism.

CURRENT
PRICE

EMBROIDERY HOOPS

☐ Sterling silver, no decoration, 5¼″ diameter ...   35.00
☐ Walnut and cherry, with table clamp, hand-
   made, Shaker, 6¼″ diameter 120.00
☐ Wood, round, hand-made, 16″ diameter 9.00

Emeries

🌸🌸🌸🌸🌸🌸🌸🌸🌸🌸🌸

An emery, also known as an emery bag, emery ball, straw-berry, or needle cleaner, looks like a small pincushion (usually about one inch to two inches). It is filled with emery powder, graphite powder, or very fine sand. This fine powdery filling serves as a perfect medium to clean and smooth needles or pins that have become rusty or dirty. It also serves to sharpen needles or pins that have become dull.

The emery is always made of fabric but can vary in design from a plain ball to a delicate silver leaf. The term "strawberry" comes from the fact that this was by far the most popular shape in which emeries were made. They were also quite often incorporated into the design of the pincushion they were attached to. Today these wonderful little tools are still being used, and can be just as lovely.

Emeries are listed alphabetically by their shape.

CURRENT
PRICE

ACORN

☐ Brown linen, sterling silver leaf top 45.00

CAT

☐ Black velvet 30.00

ROUND

☐ Pillbox form, metal rim 24.00
☐ Red velvet, sterling silver cap top 35.00

STRAWBERRY

☐ Red, ornate sterling silver cap top 45.00
☐ Red, sterling silver leaf top, 1″ 45.00
☐ Red and white polka dot, sterling silver cap
   top, eighteenth century, ¾″ 95.00

Furniture

❀❀❀❀❀❀❀❀❀❀

Work tables, work stands, footstools and chairs were pieces of furniture that had been made throughout the centuries to keep the implements for sewing and needlework well protected and close at hand. These pieces were built with drawers, fabric bags and other compartments that would conveniently hold every tool being used. However, as their name implies, all these pieces had a dual purpose. The chair, for example, could have a lift-up seat as its compartment for storage. The work table could also hold a lamp or decorative objects.

Furniture is listed alphabetically by the wood of which it is made.

CURRENT
PRICE

BIRCH, TABLES AND STANDS

☐ Federal style, one drawer, circa 1840, 17½″ × 27½″ 200.00

☐ Federal, square legs, circa 1800, 27″ square ... 450.00

Sewing stand. Solid mixed woods, dark finish, clear glass knobs, top lift, 27″ high × 16″ wide × 9½″ deep, $95.00.

CURRENT
PRICE

CHERRY TABLE

☐ Federal style, one drawer, circa 1840, 18″ ×
28¾″ 225.00

LACQUER STAND

☐ Chinese, overall decoration, lyre legs, circa
  1820 .... 1200.00

MAPLE TABLES AND STANDS

☐ Bird's eye, lift top, simulated drawer front,
  ivory pulls, tapered legs with cross stretchers,
  16½" × 23" × 30" 200.00
☐ Folding hinged legs on maple top 90.00
☐ Tiger, two-drawer 295.00

MAHOGANY TABLES AND STANDS

☐ American, circa 1800, 27" high 650.00
☐ Empire, drop leaf, circa 1835, 20" × 27" 280.00
☐ Empire, American, drop leaf, circa 1830,
  29" 270.00
☐ Empire, English, drop leaf, circa 1840, 37" ×
  29½" 400.00
☐ Empire, American, nineteenth century,
  28¼" 285.00
☐ Empire, R. Pierce, drop leaf, circa 1830, 27" .. 1100.00
☐ Federal, solid and veneer, two-drawer, 17" 450.00
☐ Federal, solid and veneer, two-drawer, pull out
  basket, 28" × 11" × 15" 600.00
☐ Federal, carved leaves, circa 1790, 30" 7500.00
☐ Federal, octagonal top, circa 1805, 30" 6000.00
☐ Federal, one drawer, Salem, Massachusetts,
  circa 1805, 28" 2500.00
☐ George III, circa 1780, 21" × 29" 850.00
☐ Hinged top, two compartments, circa 1800,
  29" 1000.00
☐ Regency, bow front, medial drawers 1100.00

☐ Regency, work basket, circa 1820, 18″ ×
32″ 400.00
☐ Ring-turned legs, nineteenth century, 28¼″ ... 350.00
☐ Sheraton, two-drawer, turned legs, circa
1800 .... 700.00
☐ Sheraton, three center drawers, two side
compartments 550.00
☐ Three-drawer with two rounded side-top
hinged pockets, circa 1910 .... 145.00
☐ Whalebone inserts, three removable tiers, octagonal sides, diamond inlays, top whalebone
pincushion cup, Nantucket, eighteenth
century. 5900.00

MIXED WOODS, TABLES AND STANDS, CHAIR

☐ Chair, one slat back, natural finish, cane seat,
27″ high 350.00
☐ Cherry and pine, Shaker, circa 1800, 21″ ×
20″ 650.00
☐ Cherry and mahogany, drop leaf, two-drawer,
turned legs, 29″ × 18″ × 35″ 300.00
☐ Mahogany and maple panels (bird's eye) 500.00
☐ Mahogany and maple, Massachusetts, circa
1800s, 31″ 1000.00
☐ Mahogany and satinwood, Federal, Salem,
Massachusetts, circa 1800, 19″ 5250.00
☐ Maple, pine and poplar, 27½″ 350.00
☐ Pine, red stained with butternut drawer
fronts, natural fold outs, Shaker, circa 1800s,
31½″ × 42½″ × 12½″ 4200.00
☐ Pine and maple, two-drawer, 91″ long 4000.00
☐ Pine and maple, two-drawer 5000.00
☐ Unknown woods, two-drawer, drop leaf, circa
1840, 36½″ × 28½″ 380.00
☐ Unknown woods, Shenandoah Valley, fluted
legs 800.00

CURRENT
PRICE

☐ Unknown woods, one drawer with tray and
spool holders, circa 1920 .... 150.00
☐ Unknown woods, fold out work area, circa late
nineteenth century 350.00
☐ Unknown woods, sliding drawers to both
sides, pedestal stand on cabriole legs, late
nineteenth century 325.00

OAK TABLES AND STANDS

☐ Double lid, two-drawer, circa 1900 .... 185.00
☐ Double lids on sides, three-door, circa 1920 .... 175.00
☐ Folding legs, solid top 95.00
☐ Three-drawer, drop leaf on one side, 27 " ×
20 " × 44 " when open. 165.00

PAPIER-MÂCHÉ TABLE

☐ With mother-of-pearl inlays, 29 " × 28 " 650.00

PINE, TABLE AND FOOTSTOOLS

☐ Footstool with hinged lid and sewing compartment, circa 1925, Queen Anne style 35.00
☐ Footstool, box style, hinged lid 30.00
☐ Sheraton, turned legs, base shelf, country
type 180.00

ROSEWOOD TABLES AND STANDS

☐ Regency, frieze, fabric receptacle 1200.00
☐ Victorian, lyre supports, circa 1850, 31 " 400.00

WALNUT TABLES AND STANDS

☐ Drop leaf, two-drawer, spool-turned legs 245.00
☐ Neoclassical, Continental, 28 " 425.00
☐ Renaissance revival, ebonized, 30 " 375.00

Sewing table. Mixed woods, cherry finish, Lindquist Ralston, Hanson Clock Co., Rockford, IL. Removable drawers with thread pegs and concave compartments, circa 1928, $135.00.

	CURRENT PRICE
☐ Rococo revival, one drawer, curved legs, 29″	275.00
☐ Two-tier, wooden pull, Shaker, 7″ wide	300.00

WICKER STANDS

☐ Double lift tops	185.00
☐ Lift top, bamboo wicker and rattan, 29½″	245.00

Gauges

Early gauges were any tools that were used to measure the size of a loop or stitch. They were most often made of bone, ivory, wood or metal. Later, gauges came with demarcated measures in either centimeters or inches. These were used to mark hems or any distance of importance. A good example were buttonhole scissors equipped with an adjustable gauge to measure the distance from the edge of the fabric. Seam cutters also have been made with built-in gauges. Knitting, crocheting and quilting gauges have also been made.

Today, the hem gauge is the type that is most easily found as a separate implement on the market. Hem gauges are used to mark the point at which the hem of any garment must be turned up. They are still being made in many different forms and of many different materials. They have been made in wood, cast iron, steel, aluminum and more recently, in plastic. Although now they are usually quite simple, during the late 1800s they were sometimes made in engraved or embossed sterling silver.

Hem gauge. Wood adjustable measure, metal powder holder. Cast-iron gilt base, original powder in tin, $12.00.

CURRENT
PRICE

CAST IRON

☐ Circa 1910, hem gauge 10.00
☐ Marked "Pelouze," hem gauge, circa 1894 ...... 30.00
☐ Swirl top, hem gauge 17.00

STERLING SILVER

☐ Floral embossed design on circular slide, hem
  gauge 29.00
☐ Heart and roses in relief design, hem gauge 25.00
☐ Plain hem gauge 24.00

Irons

❁❁❁❁❁❁❁❁❁❁

Implements or tools for pressing or ironing clothes have been in existence for many centuries. For a period of time all clothes were placed, while slightly damp, into a linen press. The press contained a heavy wood plank attached to a mechanism which was used to press the plank down onto the clothes—hence the term "pressing." Even with the passing of the linen press, the term pressing has remained.

Hand irons have been in existence for many centuries. Earliest references to irons date from 1100. Many of these irons can be seen in museums, but can rarely be found in the marketplace. Almost all irons that are collected today date from around 1850 to 1910. Irons from this period are quite easy to obtain and come in a wide variety of types. All of the irons from this period were heated in four ways.

1. By conduction, usually by heating on top of a wood stove.
2. By liquid or gas, such as natural gas, alcohol or gasoline, that was stored in an external container attached to the

Fluting irons. *Left.* Three-piece, marked on base, "Shepard Hardware Company/Buffalo, NY," $75.00. *Right.* Two-piece cast iron, waffle top handle, "C.W. Whitefield/Syracuse NY," "The best," $40.00.

iron. The liquid or gas was then fed into the body of the iron where it was burned.

3. By a heated metal slug placed in the body of the iron.
4. By burning solids, such as charcoal or coal, which were placed in the body of the iron.

The iron plays a very important role in accomplishing a task. Unfortunately, it is obvious that most irons of this period were quite heavy and made ironing difficult and time consuming. Thankfully, by around 1910 the electric iron began to take over the market. As of now there has been very little interest shown in collecting this modern iron. But keep in mind that knowing what a future collectible may be is part of the fun. Also, when adding any iron to a collection be aware that some irons, particularly miniature ones, have often been reproduced.

Irons are listed alphabetically by the heating medium.

CURRENT
PRICE

ALCOHOL

- ☐ Combination fluting, flat and round, cylinder tank, American, circa 1880 .... 75.00
- ☐ Hawkes Flat-Iron Company, Chicago, Patent 1903, "Comfort," cast aluminum cylinder tank, single row of vent holes, turned wood handle. 32.00
- ☐ Omega Company of Thuringia, Germany, cylinder tank, double row of vent holes in body, flared wood handle 40.00
- ☐ "Jubilee," Patent 1889, cylinder tank, arch-shaped wood handle 34.00
- ☐ Sears Roebuck Company, "Laundry Maid," double bell-shaped tank, single row of vent holes, turned wood handle 30.00
- ☐ Sun Manufacturing Company, cylinder tank, ribbed body, wood handle 20.00

CHARCOAL

- ☐ Bless and Drake, face on rear damper, front chimney, fluted side plate 62.00
- ☐ Cast iron, two side dampers, double-spouted .. 55.00
- ☐ Chinese, open bronze pan, Chinese inscriptions on sides of pan, plain handle 85.00
- ☐ Combination flat and fluter, fluter in handle, American, circa 1880 .... 65.00
- ☐ "Eclipse," Patent 1903, single damper, two-tier top with handle 35.00
- ☐ European, bird latch in front, sawtooth ventilation holes under high top, multiple holes in body 85.00
- ☐ European, side spout, heat shield under wood handle, single damper 38.00
- ☐ India, rear hinge, bronze, large vent holes in body, wood-turned handle, wide thin base 95.00

CURRENT
PRICE

☐ "Ne Plus Ultra," two side dampers, adjustable
top vent holes, circa 1900 .... 35.00
☐ Paguel, cast iron 45.00

CONDUCTION, EGG OR BALL

☐ Cast iron, sleeve iron, long handle 40.00
☐ Cast iron, egg shape at end of long rod 54.00

CONDUCTION, FLAT (SAD)

☐ A.C.W., cast iron 10.00
☐ "Best," rocker type fluter, two-piece 35.00
☐ Carver, Racine, Wisconsin, Patent 1898, com-
bination flat iron and reversible fluter, double-
pointed 50.00
☐ Cast iron, detachable handle, sleeve iron 25.00
☐ Cast iron, double-pointed, unknown maker 14.00
☐ Cast iron, fluter, miniature, $1\frac{3}{8}'' \times 2''$
rocker 54.00
☐ Cast iron, keystone shield 10.00
☐ Cast iron, miniature, double-pointed 25.00
☐ Cast iron, miniature, flat iron, $1\frac{3}{4}''$ 45.00
☐ Cast iron, miniature, sleeve iron, $1''$ 30.00
☐ Cast iron, miniature, sleeve iron, $1\frac{3}{4}''$ 45.00
☐ Cast iron, miniature, sleeve iron, $1\frac{7}{8}''$,
American 45.00
☐ Cast iron, miniature, $2''$ 40.00
☐ Colebrookdale, flat iron with egg-shaped iron
at end, wooden handle, $12''$ long 35.00
☐ Colebrookdale, marked "C" in shield 12.00
☐ Colebrookdale, marked "C" in shield, "#20,"
tailor's iron, slender body, heavy 27.00
☐ Colebrookdale, pointed at both ends, detach-
able handle with central latch 10.00

CURRENT
PRICE

☐ Colebrookdale, flat egg-shaped sleeve iron,
wooden handle 35.00

☐ Dover Manufacturing Company, detachable
cover over cast "Asbestos" signed base,
child's, green handle, 1½″ × 3½″ 38.00

☐ Dover Manufacturing Company, detachable
cover over cast "Asbestos" signed base,
pointed at both ends 19.00

☐ Dover Manufacturing Company, detachable
cover over cast "Asbestos" signed base, sleeve
iron 25.00

☐ Enterprise Manufacturing Company, detachable arched handle, pointed at both ends 13.00

☐ Enterprise Manufacturing Company, "Star,"
cast iron with holes in circular handle 15.00

☐ French, cantilever, hooked cast iron handle 25.00

☐ French, low base with narrow rim 10.00

☐ Grand Union Tea Company, Bentwood detach-
able handle, sleeve iron, 8″ long 45.00

☐ "HUB," pointed sleeve iron 50.00

☐ Kenrick, cast iron, English 10.00

☐ Knapp, M.H., Bay City, Missouri, combination
fluter and flat iron, cast iron, internal fluter,
hinged at front, 6½″ long 100.00

☐ Knapp, combination fluter and flat iron, fluter
unlatches from iron, 1870 .... 100.00

☐ Mrs. Potts, pointed at both ends, detachable
arched handle 10.00

☐ "Ober," cast iron, ribbed handle 20.00

☐ Streeter, "Sensible," pointed at one end, detachable handle 24.00

☐ Streeter, pointed at both ends, rear latch
mechanism for detachable handle 20.00

☐ "Wapak," cast iron 14.00

☐ Wrought iron, long, slender body 30.00

Left. Flat sleeve iron. Cast-iron base, cast iron and wood removable handle. "Grand Union/Tea Company," 8″ long, $45.00. *Right.* Flat iron, detachable wood and cast-iron handle, upward curve on one end of base, Philadelphia, PA "Enterprise," $20.00.

CURRENT
PRICE

CONDUCTION, FLUTERS

☐ "Best," rocker handle, two-piece 40.00
☐ "American" 70.00
☐ Cast iron, one-piece, hinged 55.00
☐ Cast iron, Patent August 2, 1870 .... 70.00
☐ Machine, crank type, brass rollers, Patent
  1875 .... 70.00
☐ Machine, "Crown," Philadelphia, Pennsylva-
  nia, crank type, brass rollers, table clamp,
  circa 1880 .... 75.00
☐ Machine, "Crown," Philadelphia, Pennsylva-
  nia, crank type, painted black with striping,
  circa 1880 .... 90.00

	CURRENT PRICE
☐ Machine, board with clips to hold fabric	25.00
☐ New Geneva, miniature, rocker handle, two-piece	45.00
☐ Whitfield, C.W., "Magic," Watkins, New York, cast iron, two-piece	65.00
☐ Wrought iron, wood handle, scissors, American	150.00

CONDUCTION, GOOSE (Tailor's smoothing iron generally with a goose neck or long handle)

☐ Forged handle, circa 1820	65.00
☐ Hand wrought, spiral-turned handle	30.00
☐ Twists around the handle, 11¼", eighteenth century	85.00

GASOLINE

☐ Akron Lamp Company, plastic handle, triangular tank, pump in handle	28.00
☐ Coleman, blue enameled wood and plastic handle, round rear tank, pressure pump	30.00
☐ Coleman, plastic handle, round rear tank, pressure pump	25.00
☐ Coleman, wood and plastic handle, round rear tank, pressure pump	30.00

ELECTRIC

☐ Wolverine	10.00

NATURAL GAS

☐ Clefton Pumping and Heating Iron, turned-wood handle, vertical vent holes in base, chimney in front, circa 1900	40.00

☐ "I Want You," turned-wood handle, flexible
hose for gas, round vent holes in base, pointed
at both ends, 1913 .... 30.00

☐ Round vent holes in base, flexible hose for gas
in the back, round vent holes in base 30.00

SLUG

☐ American Machine Company, "Star," fluter
machine, cast-iron base, crank type 75.00

☐ American Machine Company, fluting iron,
crank type, two-piece 50.00

☐ Austrian, brass, turned-wood handle, bullet
nose, door at back 95.00

☐ "Best," two-piece fluting iron, rocker type 40.00

☐ Bless and Drake, combination fluter and flat
iron 55.00

☐ Cast iron, turned-wood handle, knife gate
door 80.00

☐ Danish, brass, handle with iron work on sup-
ports, 5″ long 115.00

☐ English, brass, miniature, 2¾″ long 150.00

☐ English, brass, turned-wood handle, knife gate
door, turned posts 125.00

☐ European, brass, goffering iron, marble base,
double barrel brass tubes 350.00

☐ European, brass, wrought iron handle, bullet
nose, knife gate door 80.00

☐ European, box iron (knife gate door, with spi-
ral design inside) 75.00

☐ "Geneva Hand Fluter," rocker type, two-piece,
1866 .... 45.00

☐ Kendrick, "S," goffering iron, single bullet-
shaped barrel, with stand 75.00

☐ Knapp, combination fluter and flat iron, fluter
held to flat iron with latch, circa 1870 .... 55.00

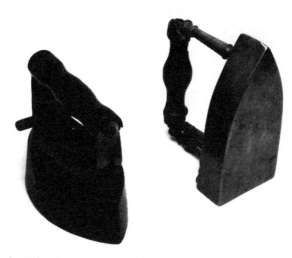

Left. Cast slug iron. Wood turned handle, $80.00. *Right.* Brass slug iron with wood turned handle and brass support, $80.00.

	CURRENT PRICE
☐ "Mrs. Potts," interchangeable handles with three nickel-plated slugs, circa 1908	60.00
☐ "Mrs. Streeters Gem Polisher," American, circa 1900	60.00
☐ "New Victoria," pleating board of sheet metal	20.00
☐ Scandinavian, brass, ornate brass posts, engraved top, 6″ long	200.00
☐ Swan, miniature, black paint, American, 3″ long	75.00
☐ Whitfield, C.W., fluting iron, roller, two pieces	45.00
☐ Wrought iron, fluting scissors	45.00
☐ Wrought iron, goffering iron	100.00
☐ Wrought iron, knife gate door with spiral design inside, 6″ long, American	80.00

Cast slug iron with turned wood handle. "Dover/No. 922/ Sad Iron," 4¾″, $45.00.

CURRENT
PRICE

MISCELLANEOUS, SPECIAL-PURPOSE IRONS

☐ Hat iron, for hat brims and special shapes 30.00
☐ Polishing iron, with rounded bottom, cast
    iron 40.00
☐ Shoulder iron, with rounded bottom, triangu-
    lar shape 40.00
☐ Sleeve iron, with slender bullet shape to reach
    into small areas 30.00

Kits

ൠൠൠൠൠൠൠൠൠൠ

The term "kits" is used in this book to refer to the very small boxes or containers that were fitted with the tools or implements needed to perform a needlework task. They were made to be carried around in the purse or bag or to be tucked into traveling cases. They were a great convenience when immediate repairs were in order. In fact, these kits are still quite popular. The most common sewing kits contained a spool with one or more colors of thread, a needle and pin holder, one or two safety pins, perhaps a thimble and small scissors. Special kits were made, however, to perform specific tasks such as darning, which naturally included a miniature darning egg.

Toward the late 1800s and into the 1900s, the little sewing kit became a very popular form of advertising giveaways. Many companies, both large and small, had their logos on sewing kits. Local businesses also used this form for advertising.

Sewing kits are very charming, but since the various objects fitted into the kit are very small, they do tend to get lost. It is best to look for kits that are complete and with their original tools intact.

Advertising kits. *Left.* Yellow plastic fitted with thread, needle holder, thimble, "Bowman's Products Co., Cleveland 3 Ohio/Oakland CA" in blue ink, 2½" long, $6.00. *Right.* Chrome, local service station on paper label covered with plastic, $5.00.

Sewing kits are listed by the material of which they are made, with the exception that advertising kits are listed separately.

CURRENT
PRICE

ADVERTISING

☐ Calvert Whiskey, bottle shape, plastic, 1940s	8.00
☐ Calvert Whiskey, yellow enameled logo, 1¾" ..	13.00
☐ Cinderella Orange, J.F. Lazier Manufacturing Company, Inc., chrome	9.00
☐ Coats, J.P., paper, lithograph logo	18.00
☐ Elsie the Cow, Borden, case fitted for darning	12.00
☐ Gain Owensboro	7.00
☐ Local, grocery store, New York, plastic	6.00
☐ Local, tailor shop, Vermont	7.00
☐ Local, shoe store, Wisconsin	6.00
☐ Lydia Pinkham, chrome, inscribed logo	12.00
☐ Lydia Pinkham, metal, inscribed company name and slogan	12.00

CURRENT
PRICE

- ☐ Lydia Pinkham, fitted with tatting needle and thread, tape measure 45.00
- ☐ Sealtest Ice Cream, cone-shaped 20.00
- ☐ Singer Sewing Machines, chrome 14.00
- ☐ White Sewing Machines, celluloid 15.00

BRASS

- ☐ Bullet shape, fitted with needles, thread and thimble, late 18.00
- ☐ Fitted with ivory needlecase and threader 85.00
- ☐ Tube-shape with enamel floral decoration, fitted with needles, thread, safety pins 15.00

ENAMEL

- ☐ Rose decoration, opalescent top, 2¼", circa 1920 .... 70.00

LEATHER

- ☐ "Ladies Companion," fitted with stainless steel thimble, scissors, needle case, and punch, stainless steel hinges on oval box, 3" high, circa late 1700s 110.00
- ☐ Needlepoint top, Austrian 25.00

Travel kit. Fitted with scissor, bodkin, needlebook, thread and pins. Leather with needlepointed insert in pastel floral, Germany, 3¼" long, $15.00.

CURRENT
PRICE

PAPER

☐ Heavy cardboard, lithograph picture of Crystal
Palace, souvenir, fitted with thimble, needles,
and pincushion, lined 60.00

SILVER, PLATE

☐ Embossed dragon, attached beaded chain,
3″ 35.00

SILVER, STERLING

☐ Embossed floral decoration 80.00

Knitting Tools

❧❧❧❧❧❧❧❧❧❧

Knitting is simply the process of pulling one loop of yarn through another. This loop through a loop stitch can be varied by crossing, turning, skippings, and combinations of stitches to produce many textures, patterns and designs. In fact, most design patterns used today have their origins in very early history.

Knitted garments and fabric have been recorded through history since early Arabic and Egyptian times. At its beginnings, and for many centuries, knitting, like weaving, was a man's work. In Europe, boys became apprentice knitters. They served a long apprenticeship learning and studying and then, if they passed the test, could become Masters in the Guild. All commercial knitted fabric was produced by men. Hand weaving and knitting were the only way of producing fabric until the advent of power-driven looms during the nineteenth century.

This is not to say that women did not knit. They probably always have. They just did not do it commercially. Knitting by women was done for home use. In America, however, things were quite different. Here, knitting has always been considered a woman's job. The Guild system never took hold in America. Young girls were taught as a part of their curriculum at "ladies' schools" how to knit, and were expected to produce a sampler. Most of these samplers were approximately six inches wide and a yard long, exhibiting a succession of patterns. Unfortunately, unlike embroidery samplers, very few of these samplers survive. Any found at this date should be carefully preserved and any from the eighteenth century should be considered museum pieces.

Today we think of most knitting as using yarn (wool, synthetic, cotton) but knitting can be done using any material or filament that is produced in sufficient lengths. Outstanding pieces of knitting have been produced using silk threads in many colors and spun gold. The only tools needed for knitting are knitting needles and yarn. Knitting needles are rounded, slim, tools that are tapered at one end and usually have a knob on the other end. They come in various sizes to achieve different-sized loops. Early knitting needles were made of materials at hand such as ivory, bone, whale ivory and wood. Additional tools that have been used are needles pointed at both ends, knitting needle gauges (to determine the standardized size of the needle), row counters (to count the number of rows to a pattern) and the sample gauges (to determine the knitter's stitch to the actual size of the pattern). Knitting needles have come in fitted cases with needles of all sizes.

CURRENT
PRICE

CASE ONLY

☐ Tin with brushwork design, circa 1830, 9¼″ ..   55.00

KNITTING NEEDLES

☐ Bone, plain, pair 20.00
☐ Whale ivory and ebony, acorn finials, circa
1850, pair, 13½″ long 220.00

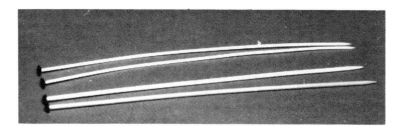

Knitting needles. Two pair, ivory with dyed black heads, 13½″ long, $24.00 pair.

CURRENT
PRICE

☐ Wood, dark finish, whale ivory top acorn,
turned, mid nineteenth century, pair, 13½″
long 200.00

KNITTING NEEDLES IN CASE

☐ Metal case, with lithograph tin picture, cylin-
der, circa 1900, five pair 45.00
☐ Moire over wood, two sides fold out, fitted
with English needles and crochet hooks, row
counter, bodkin, and tapestry needle, 7″ x
12″ 35.00
☐ Wood case, cone shaped, sterling silver pair ... 85.00
☐ Wood case, cylinder, American, five pairs 40.00

Magazines

❦❦❦❦❦❦❦❦❦❦

Magazines have always reflected daily life. They have chronicled the society and history of their time.

At first thought, it might be difficult to understand why magazines would be of interest to a collector of sewing and needlework memorabilia, but for more than one hundred years, magazines have been published strictly for the woman's market. These magazines, whether they are general or devoted specifically to sewing and needlework, contain a wealth of related material. The covers may depict women engaged in needlework or sewing. Advertisements for tools used in sewing and needlework are abundant. Patterns and designs for sewing, knitting, embroidery, crewel, crochet, in fact, every form of needlework, abound. The covers, the advertisements and the patterns and designs give a very accurate picture of the style of dress that was in fashion at any particular time.

Probably the most popular collectibles of magazine memorabilia in the sewing and needlework area at the present time are the colored prints taken from *Godey's Lady's Book*.

Literally thousands of these lovely prints have been separately framed.

Artist-produced magazine covers, both signed and unsigned, are very collectible and can be framed to make an interesting and decorative addition to a collection. Advertisements from these magazines, again artist-produced or photographically produced, can be very interesting and charming. They, too, can be framed as decorative accessories. It should be noted that if a magazine cover, or any pages, are to be framed they should be placed on an acid-free mat and never glued for the best preservation possible. The same is true when buying an already framed piece. Keep in mind that a piece that is already framed will, of course, be more expensive.

As a rule, artist-signed covers will be the most expensive and generally range from $10–$50 per cover. Unsigned artist covers depicting fashion are in the $9–$12 range in a large size and $6–$8 range in a small size. These are prices for unframed material, in clean and crisp condition.

Magazine tear sheets (pages with advertisements) depicting fashion generally range from $2–$4 with colored ads and pre-1930 ads at the high end of the range. Tear sheets depicting household products generally range from $1–$5. Again, colored ads and early ads will be at the high end of the range. Artist-signed colored ads would be even higher, generally ranging from $4–$12. These are prices for unframed material, in clean and crisp condition.

Complete magazines are the least expensive way to collect this material. Many can be found at flea markets, garage sales, and auctions in box lots, and the collector can have the fun of looking through them.

Magazines are listed alphabetically by the name.

McCall's Needlework and Crafts, Spring/Summer, 1961,
$ .50; *Woman's Day*, 1961, $ .50.

CURRENT
PRICE

AMERICAN NEEDLEWOMAN

☐ Pre-1940 .... $ .50.

COMFORT

☐ A needlecraft magazine, issues from 1935 to
1942 .... 9.00

GODEY'S LADY'S BOOK

☐ All illustrations intact, bound, year run for
1842 .... 50.00
☐ Framed print 17.00–
24.00

CURRENT
PRICE

GOOD HOUSEKEEPING

- ☐ 1930 .... 1.45
- ☐ 1941 .... 1.25
- ☐ 1945 .... 1.25

HARPER'S BAZAAR

- ☐ 1883, bound, year run for 1883 .... 80.00
- ☐ 1917, cover by Erte 30.00

HOME ARTS

- ☐ Needlecraft magazine, 1935–1942 .... 9.00
- ☐ 1930 .... 2.50

HOME FRIEND

- ☐ 1929–1932, 27 issues 25.00

HOME NEEDLEWORK

- ☐ Year run for 1906 .... 8.00

HOUSEWIFE

- ☐ 1912, one issue 4.00

LADIES HOME JOURNAL

- ☐ Harrison Fisher covers, five different
  issues 75.00
- ☐ 1889, Christmas issue 10.00
- ☐ 1891, November, brownies 10.00
- ☐ 1891, complete year 75.00
- ☐ 1895, Christmas issue, Gibson and Green-
  away illustrations 15.00
- ☐ 1896, July, Maxfield Parrish cover 15.00

	CURRENT PRICE
☐ 1898, Christmas issue	10.00
☐ 1903, February, Maxfield Parrish cover	18.00
☐ 1910, January, Lettie Lane paper doll	12.50
☐ 1910, February	15.00
☐ 1911, March	16.00
☐ 1912, April	16.00
☐ 1913, December	20.00
☐ 1916, December, Maxfield Parrish advertisement	25.00
☐ 1917, Red Cross, nurse and dog	18.00
☐ 1920, December, Maxfield Parrish advertisement	25.00
☐ 1925, July, Maxfield Parrish advertisement	25.00
☐ 1926, December	8.00
☐ 1927, August, Rose O'Neill, Kewpieville	17.00
☐ 1930, March, Maxfield Parrish	30.00
☐ 1931, January, Maxfield Parrish	35.00
☐ 1940, July	1.50

McCALL'S

☐ 1875	11.00
☐ 1930	3.50

NEEDLECRAFT

☐ 1909–1919, various issues	2.00
☐ 1917–1927, lot of 40 issues	45.00
☐ 1919, February, Rose O'Neill Jello ad and Cream of Wheat ads	20.00
☐ 1920, Christmas issue, Santa Claus Cream of Wheat ad in color	9.00
☐ 1920s, five issues with full page Cream of Wheat ads	35.00
☐ 1920–1930, various issues	2.00

Tear sheet from *McCall's*. Fashions from 1968, fun but no value.

	CURRENT PRICE
☐ 1927	2.00
☐ 1939	1.00

NEEDLEWORK

☐ 1926	8.50

NEEDLEWORK AND CROCHET PATTERNS

☐ 1910–1930, lot of 27 issues	40.00

CURRENT
PRICE

NEW IDEA WOMAN

☐ 1900 .... 8.00

POPULAR NEEDLEWORK

☐ 1970s, various issues .... .35

STITCH AND SEW

☐ 1970s, various issues .... .40

WOMAN'S CIRCLE

☐ 1966, Christmas issue 4.00

WOMAN'S DAY

☐ 1960s, various issues .... .35

WOMAN'S HOME COMPANION

☐ 1890, January 5.00
☐ 1902, August 4.00
☐ 1938, February, Norman Rockwell
   illustration 8.00
☐ 1938, August, Norman Rockwell illustration ... 8.00
☐ 1941, January, Norman Rockwell
   illustration 8.00

WOMAN'S WORLD

☐ 1936, February 1.50

Needles

❀❀❀❀❀❀❀❀❀❀

A needle is an implement that is pointed at one end and has an eye (or hole) at the other end. The thread to be used, for whatever purpose, can now be passed through the material to be worked.

Needles have been in existence since civilization began. The first needles would have been made out of whatever materials were available. Eskimos and early Indian tribes used thorns, fishbones, whalebone and ivory. Later, bronze and steel were commonly used. The manufacture of steel needles, almost as we know them today, was introduced in China very early (several centuries B.C.) and by the sixteenth century they were being produced in the Near East and Spain. Needles were also made in Europe by craftsmen. At that time, needlemaking was an art, a specialized craft. In Colonial America, steel needles had to be imported from Europe for there were virtually no needlemakers. It was not until the late 1890s that the manufacture of needles began to appear. Needles were considered a very precious possession, and were well cared for by the owner.

At this time needles are not in particularly high demand as a collectible. However, for the collector they represent a very broad spectrum of the needleworker's and sewer's art. They are small and easy to display. They have been made in many forms for many different specific tasks.

A partial list would include the following (also see Needle Books):

Blunt needle, round eye, short, thick and strong, used by tailors and stay makers.

Bookbinder's needle, long with round points.

Calyx-eye needle, self-threading with a slit at the top.

Candlewick needle, thick and long, big eye.

Chenille needle, short, large eye, sharp point.

Crewel needle, elongated eye, comes in same sizes as "sharp."

Curved needle, normal size eye, curved almost to semi-circle, comes in various sizes and thicknesses, used for upholstery and awkward sewing jobs.

Darning needle, long with big eye.

Mattress needle, double-pointed, eye at one end, 6″ to 8″ long, used to make tufts in mattress.

Pack needle, large, strong, to sew up shipping packs.

Quilting needle, short, sharp, pointed, in sizes 7–8.

Self-threading needles, see Calyx-eye needle.

Sewing machine needles, various sizes.

Sharp needle, the most common kind of needle to be found; they are medium length with a sharp point and a small eye, sizes vary from thick (05) to very fine (12).

Straw needle, very long and fine, used in millinery and some types of embroidery (beading).

Tapestry needle, short, large eye, blunt tip.

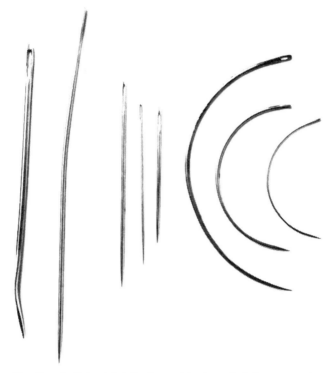

Needles. *Left to right.* Sacks and bags, upholstery, carpets, sail makers, tapestry, upholstery, upholstery, mattress.

Needle and
Pin Cases

❀❀❀❀❀❀❀❀❀❀

Needles and pins, in one form or another, have been in existence for many, many centuries. Indeed, they have probably been around for as long as clothing has been worn and needed to be mended or held together. Although needles and pins have always been considered a necessity, at one time they were also considered to be very precious, because they were difficult and expensive to obtain. Great care was taken to keep them safe and covered. Hence, needle and pin cases (or boxes) were devised.

The early Eskimo and Indian tribes carved needle cases out of the same materials from which their needles and pins were made. In early Anglo-Saxon days and later, the needle case was often attached to the chatelaine (see Chatelaines). Later, simple tubes were devised through which the needle could be drawn threaded through a piece of fabric and pulled up through the tube. During the eighteenth century needle and pin cases became much more elaborate and intricately

Ebony needle and pin case. Inlaid very narrow border of mother-of-pearl, 3¾" × 2¼", $25.00.

worked, while in the nineteenth century they took on fanciful forms. During the twentieth century these lovely little cases have gone out of fashion. With the advent of cheaper needles and pins, the cases have become virtually useless. Later examples of needle and pin cases or holders will be concentrated in advertising pieces such as needle books.

Needle and pin cases are listed alphabetically by the material from which they are made.

CURRENT
PRICE

BAKELITE

☐ Coke bottle shape, unscrews in the middle 20.00
☐ Cylinder, with tassel on bottom, thimble top,
Germany 8.00
☐ Penguin, black and white, 3" 7.00

	CURRENT PRICE

BONE

☐ Cylinder, plain 25.00
☐ Fish shape, carved, handle screws out of mouth 30.00

BRASS

☐ Cylinder, plain 18.00
☐ Golden Casket, Thomas Savage, England 95.00

CARDBOARD

☐ Cylinder, "Happy Home," complete with gold eye needles, circa 1920, 6″ x 3½″ 19.00

CHINA

☐ Pincushion top, mirror under lid, 2½″ x 1½″, Japan 9.00

HORN

☐ Cylinder, carved, opens at one end 60.00
☐ Cylinder, carved, opens at both ends 65.00

IVORY

☐ Book shape, with fabric pages 95.00
☐ Cylinder, plain 65.00
☐ Cylinder, carved basketweave pattern 85.00
☐ Gavel shape 90.00
☐ Fish shape 95.00
☐ Parasol shape, 4⅜″ 125.00
☐ Pea Pod shape, 4″ 165.00
☐ Umbrella shape, opens to fabric pages 125.00

FABRIC

☐ Beaded, rose pattern, fabric pages, dated 1839 .... 95.00

☐ Embroidered, fabric pages, late 9.00
☐ Needlepoint, book form, fabric pages 45.00

LEATHER

☐ Black, gold embossed, fold over, fabric-
embroidered pages for pins, 2″ x 1⅞″ 45.00

LEATHERETTE

☐ Book shape, gold embossed advertising, 5″ x
2½″, advertising, circa 1900 .... 8.50

METAL

☐ Egg shape, gold colored 20.00
☐ Fish shape, green, painted, 4¼″ 60.00

MOTHER-OF-PEARL

☐ Cylinder, opens at one end 20.00
☐ Cylinder, opens at both ends 22.00
☐ Carved, circa nineteenth century, 3½″ 85.00
☐ Advertising giveaway, Food Fair 1.50

PAPER

☐ Advertising giveaway, Food Fair 1.50

PEWTER

☐ Key shape 45.00

SILVER

☐ Chinese, cylinder, 2″ 105.00
☐ Mexican, cylinder 25.00

CURRENT
PRICE

STERLING SILVER

☐ Cylinder, embossed design of pigs 75.00
☐ Cylinder, embossed mirror back, holds 24
   pins 85.00
☐ Cylinder, embossed scroll work design 70.00
☐ Cylinder, embossed scroll, leaf and floral
   design 65.00
☐ Cylinder, opens at the middle, plain 35.00
☐ Cylinder, opens at both ends, plain 32.00
☐ Key shape, pewter top 80.00

TIN

☐ Boyd, advertising, slide top, 1912 .... 8.00
☐ Black and green painted 20.00
☐ Harper's Helix Needles, advertising, with as-
   sorted size needles, England 15.00
☐ Harper's Self-Threading Needles, advertising,
   with assorted size needles, England 18.00
☐ Pin-pierced pattern, Germany 12.00

TOLE

☐ Cylinder, black ground, yellow and red deco-
   ration, 9¾" 80.00

TORTOISE SHELL

☐ Cylinder, plain 110.00
☐ Trunk shape 125.00

WHALEBONE

☐ Fluted with open work decoration, 1½"
   square 110.00
☐ Scrimshaw, early nineteenth century 140.00

WOOD

- ☐ Acorn shape, hand-carved, top screws off,
  2¾ " 22.00
- ☐ Barrel shape, mechanical, Germany 25.00
- ☐ Carved, silk-lined, circa 1870, 2½ " 55.00
- ☐ Columbian darning egg, opens to needle
  case 55.00
- ☐ Ebony, with inlaid mother-of-pearl, 3¾" x
  2¼ " 30.00
- ☐ Egg shape, sandalwood, pierced knob 65.00
- ☐ Poplar, Shaker, with velvet pincushion and
  strawberry emery 195.00
- ☐ Tankard shape, with revolving top 19.00
- ☐ Turned shape, 9½ " 45.00
- ☐ Urn shape, mechanical 18.00
- ☐ Vegetable shape, carved, 3¾ " x 1¼ " 70.00

Needle Books

❧❧❧❧❧❧❧❧❧❧❧

Needle books are folders, usually made of paper, that open to display from one to several foil or fabric paste-on pieces that are perforated in two double rows through which needles can be individually slipped. Originally, needle books came with a supply of various sized needles. Most of these were made as advertising giveaways. Many of the early needle books had very colorful lithograph pictures on the front and back. The foil paper inside was brightly colored, usually in red, green, blue and gold.

Like many advertising items, the pictures on needle books give an accurate picture of the fashion, hairstyles and lifestyles of the time they were printed. They are of interest to any collector. Likewise, needle books made to commemorate events such as fairs, expositions or centennials are also fascinating. This type of needle book is harder to find, but not necessarily more expensive than the advertising needle book.

Needle books, like all paper collectibles, should be purchased in mint to very good condition. Any creases, bends

Needle books. *Liberty Sharps,* $4.00; *Bestmaid,* $6.00; *Royal,* $8.00.

or tears in the paper reduce the value considerably. Of course, needle books, are at their best if the paper has not been discolored, bent, creased or torn, and if all the original needles are intact.

Needle books are listed alphabetically by the advertiser or picture.

	CURRENT PRICE
☐ Army and Navy, picture of vintage cruiser and plane on lithograph paper cover	8.00
☐ Capital City Dairy, paper cover	8.00
☐ Century of Progress, paper cover	9.00
☐ Dirigible shape, lithograph cover	15.00
☐ Fabric in the shape of a compact, non-advertising, beaded floral design on cover, fabric pages, dated 1834	85.00

☐ Golden D "Queen Royal" Sharps, black paper folder with red, gold, green lithographed picture of queen on front, inside white paper folder printed in black for local bank 8.00

☐ Golden Eye Gotham Flyer, racing car shape, paper folder in red, yellow and green, 4½″ x 7″ 5.00

☐ Happy Home (sewing machines), paper folder, gold eye needles and needle threader, 6″ x 3½″, circa 1920 .... 18.00

☐ Happy Home, 30 assorted gold eye needles and needle threader, printed scene on paper of three women looking at piece of fabric, 4⅝″ x 3⅜″, ... 12.00

☐ Heath & Gills, Superfine Sewing Needles, black paper case, gold lettering and logo, marked "Czechoslovakia," patent August 1, 1914, 4¾″ x 2¼″ 4.00

☐ Lipton Tea, paper folder in shape of box of tea and box of tea bags, printed replicas, 5⅛″ x 4″ 5.00

☐ Milwards, H. & Sons Needles, black paper folder, black and white printed scene of sailing ship on front, fabric insert advertising Clark's O.N.T. spool cotton 3.00

☐ Milwards needles, red, black and white paper folder, fabric insert, advertising J.P. Coats Threads, Clark's Threads, Milwards needles and Crown Zipper on reverse, England 4.00

☐ Shrimpton's needles, folding case with paper advertising on top, 4″, circa 1880 .... 12.00

☐ Smith, J.A. & Sons, Improved Drilled Eyed Sharps, black paper folder with blue background and black print, fabric insert 2.00

☐ Trans-Atlantic Aeroplane, lithograph picture on paper of aviator and vintage plane, marked "Czechoslovakia" 6.00

Needle
Threaders

A needle threader is a small metal tool which is used by the seamstress or needleworker to help thread a needle more easily. Many forms have been tried through the years, but the form that seems to have survived over time is the one made with a small, round, flat handle (about the size of a nickel or quarter). This can easily be held with the thumb and forefinger. At the bottom of the handle a very fine wire loop, generally in the shape of an elongated diamond, is attached. The loop is passed through the eye of the needle, the thread is passed through the loop and the loop is then pulled back through the needle, carrying with it the thread.

Generally the needle threader has been made of very thin steel, aluminum, or brass. Unless the collector encounters a very early needle threader, the price of the threader is generally determined by its value as an advertising item. Many were produced as giveaways for companies and local con-

Hexe blue and white plastic needle threader. Original box, 2⅛" high, $2.00.

cerns. Unfortunately, since they were very fragile (the metal and the wires were very thin), the item was not very durable. Many have been made, but not many have survived the test of time. They were also sometimes part of another sewing or needlework tool. For example, thimbles could have an attached needle threader.

	CURRENT PRICE
☐ Brass, round handle embossed with floral design	30.00
☐ Brass, plain handle	10.00
☐ Coats, J.P. (thread), logo on handle	6.00
☐ Coats, J.P., spool-shape handle with logo	9.00
☐ Clark's (thread), plain round handle	8.00
☐ Prudential Life Insurance, plain round handle	6.00
☐ Prudential Life Insurance, enameled tin with lithograph picture	10.00

Pincushions

❧❧❧❧❧❧❧❧❧❧❧

As long as needles and pins have been in use, there have been pincushions. They have come in a variety of shapes and sizes to serve the needs of the needleworker. One purpose of the pincushion is strictly utilitarian, and that is to protect the points of the needles and pins. In order to do this, they have traditionally been stuffed with materials such as sawdust, kapok, cotton or foam. Another purpose of the pincushion is convenience. As a holder, the needleworker's pins and needles could always be nearby while working.

Since pincushions were used and therefore seen with regularity, they have also been decorative items in the home. Pincushions can be found in almost every style. It was particularly fashionable to have a pincushion in the style of the needlework technique that was popular at the time. For example, Victorian times produced heavily beaded, patchwork and velvet pincushions. Today we find pincushions being made in counted cross stitch and bargello. Pincushions made in figural forms were also popular and could be quite extravagant. They could be found in a

Pincushion cover. White and very pale pink embroidery on white, 13½″ x 8½″, $14.00.

variety of metals, wood, celluloid, China, bisque or papier-mâché. The pincushion was usually very cleverly incorporated into the figure. For example, one very popular figural form for a pincushion was the half-doll. In this instance, the doll's skirt was actually a pincushion. These are extremely collectible today.

Another form of pincushion was the pincushion cover. These consisted of two pieces of fabric that could be stuffed and then joined by a frill of a fringe. They were frequently embroidered, creweled, or otherwise decorated on the top cover. They often found their place on the "toilet table" for guests or household members to use for quick mends or repairs.

Pincushions were also found as a part of other sewing and needlework tools. Many clamps and most sewing birds had a pincushion attached. Many thread holders, work boxes and baskets, and thimble holders also had pincushions incorporated into their design.

Pincushions are listed alphabetically by their shape or form.

CURRENT
PRICE

APPLE

☐ Red satin 12.00

BASKET

☐ Ivory, 3″ x 2″, handled 85.00

BABY BOOTIE

☐ Crochet 6.00

BLACK BABY

☐ Bisque, sitting on top of pincushion, Japan,
  3″ 20.00

BLACK MAMMY

☐ Fabric, face painted on board, hanging 12.00
☐ Wooden, full figure with spool holder on each
  side, souvenir, 5½″ x 9⁵/₁₂″ 23.00

BOOT

☐ Lady's with beaded birds sitting on branch,
  very ornate 45.00

BOX

☐ Tin, velvet cushion on top, opens to mirror in-
  side, Occupied Japan 18.00

CANOE

☐ Brass, with velvet cushion 18.00

CAT

☐ Pot metal, glass eyes 20.00
☐ White metal, nodder (head moves) 25.00
☐ White metal, with bronze finish 35.00

CHAIR

☐ White metal, with velvet trim 12.00

CHICKEN

☐ Fabric, spool base, 4″ 45.00

CLOWN

☐ Fabric 17.50

DIAMOND

☐ Victorian beaded 8.00

DISC

☐ Ivory, with red velvet cushion 30.00
☐ Leather, with red velvet cushion, 1¾″ dia. 32.00

DOG

☐ Silver plate 45.00

DOLL

☐ Arms bent toward breast, 4″ 25.00
☐ Arms bent with hands behind back, pink
    dress, 2″, Germany 35.00
☐ Arms open, 6¼″, Germany 40.00
☐ Arms open, headband with feather, 3¼″,
    Germany 50.00
☐ Arms open, flowers in hair, 5¾″ 45.00
☐ Arms open, strapless dress, fan comb, 2½″,
    Germany 40.00

Pincushion. Diamond over clover shape, joined with black leather strips, leather back, Victorian, $22.00.

	CURRENT PRICE
☐ Art Deco, right hand to breast, cloche hat, 2¾", Japan	25.00
☐ Art Deco, Germany	40.00
☐ Art Deco, nude, blond marcel hair wave, 8", Germany	50.00
☐ Bisque, Germany	45.00
☐ Black hair, arm to waist, 3¾"	35.00
☐ Black hair, arms folded, 3"	30.00
☐ Black Mammy, wood face, with roll out tape measure	35.00
☐ Black Mammy, chalk torso and head	35.00
☐ Blond hair, arms open, blue dress, pink flowers in hair, 2½"	35.00
☐ Blond hair, arms open, white dress, gilt beads, Germany, 3"	30.00
☐ Blond hair, blue dress, beads in hair	28.00
☐ Blond hair, hands clasped to breast, 3¾", Germany	40.00
☐ Blond hair, one arm and hand out from body, 2¼"	35.00

	CURRENT PRICE
☐ Blond hair, papier-mâché, 3¾", Germany	32.00
☐ Blond hair, pink dress, 3½"	25.00
☐ Blue bonnet and shawl, Japan	20.00
☐ Brown hair, arms and hands at neck, green dress, 3"	35.00
☐ Brown hair, orange ribbon, strapless gown, 3¾", Japan	30.00
☐ China, with elaborate hairdo, 3", Germany	35.00
☐ Colonial lady, 11"	22.00
☐ Dutch girl, one arm out and one bent at elbow, Dutch bonnet and dress, 2½"	65.00
☐ Dutch girl, holding flowers, Dutch bonnet	22.00
☐ Flapper, arms out, 4½", Germany	125.00
☐ Flapper, black hair, red browband, 4¼", Germany	55.00
☐ Flapper, head only, 3¼", Germany	30.00
☐ Flapper, pink hat, polka dot yellow blouse	25.00
☐ Gainsborough lady, rose in hand, 4"	75.00
☐ Goebel Crown Mark, Marie Antoinette	190.00
☐ Goebel signed, arms out, 5"	195.00
☐ Gray hair, arms open with hands on hips, pink dress, 3", Germany	35.00
☐ Gray hair, bisque, 4", Germany	60.00
☐ Gray hair, full-figured, long skirt, 3½", Japan	28.00
☐ Gray hair, hand to bosom, blue ribbon, 4", Germany	40.00
☐ Gray hair, papier-mâché, painted face, 5¾"	110.00
☐ Gray hair, purple and ivory bonnet and dress, 6½", Germany	80.00
☐ Hand to hair, headband, Germany	30.00
☐ Hat trimmed with roses, 3", Japan	25.00
☐ Japanese lady, arms folded to breast holding fan, 2", Japan	22.00
☐ Japanese lady, green gown, comb in hair, 3¾", Japan	23.00
☐ Marie Antoinette, hands clasped to bosom, 3½"	35.00

CURRENT
PRICE

☐ Nude woman, holding rose 90.00
☐ Painted plaster 12.00
☐ Queen Anne era, ruffled collar, green scarf,
4″, Germany 40.00
☐ Schneider, marked, 5½″ 100.00
☐ Spanish dancer, arm to head, blue comb,
3¾″, Germany 40.00
☐ Spanish dancer, haircomb, 3″, Germany 40.00
☐ Spanish woman, hat and shawl, 4″,
Germany 35.00
☐ Victorian woman, one arm to breast, 2¼″ 28.00
☐ Victorian woman, painted features, molded
hair, 9″ 30.00

DUCK

☐ Fabric 18.00

ELEPHANT

☐ Sterling silver, blue velvet cushion 85.00
☐ White metal 18.00

FIDDLE

☐ White metal, set with tiny stones, 4¼″ 35.00

GLOBE

☐ Pedestal, tape measure rolls out of base, thimble holder 35.00

HAT

☐ Wide brim, scissor holder, sachet holder 15.00

HEART

☐ Beaded in crossed American flags, Indian 50.00
☐ Indian-beaded, 1895 .... 45.00
☐ Reed & Barton silver, ornate 90.00

Pink crochet over pink satin, 5″ long, $17.00.

	CURRENT PRICE

HITLER
☐ Cast plaster, bending over 65.00

LEG AND BOOT
☐ Fabric, 12½″ 40.00

LIBERTY BELL
☐ Metal, 1876 centennial souvenir 60.00

LION
☐ White metal, gilded, roaring 40.00

MONKEY
☐ Fabric 30.00

PARROT
☐ Fabric, yellow, green, gray 20.00

PEDESTAL BASE

☐ Ivory, with red velvet cushion, 2″ 40.00
☐ Ivory, with thread holder, 6″ 95.00

PIG

☐ Silver plate, sitting 45.00

POCKETBOOK

☐ Beaded, Victorian 25.00

RABBIT

☐ Silver plate, Victorian 75.00
☐ White metal, sitting 20.00

ROOSTER

☐ Wood, primitive 34.00

ROUND

☐ Advertising, 2¼″ 8.00
☐ Beaded, flags, Indian 40.00
☐ Beaded, birds in flight pattern, dated, 8″ 45.00
☐ Beaded, song birds in center 40.00
☐ Beaded, velvet, floral and scalloped center,
7½″ 30.00
☐ Blue velvet, fleur-de-lis decoration 185.00
☐ Brass and walnut base, velvet cushion, brass
dog at the side holds thimble 65.00
☐ Embroidered velvet, braid trim, Victorian,
7″ 22.00
☐ Patchwork, 8″ 12.00
☐ Porcelain, rose tapestry decor 155.00
☐ Sterling silver, velvet cushion 85.00

	CURRENT PRICE

SHOE OR SLIPPER

☐ Celluloid, red	8.00
☐ Cloth, high button lady's	15.00
☐ Coppertone metal, lady's, souvenir of state capital Phoenix, Arizona	30.00
☐ Gilded metal, lady's	20.00
☐ Gold scroll decoration, red velvet cushion, Occupied Japan	12.00
☐ Metal, Occupied Japan	10.00
☐ Pewter, lady's, red velvet cushion	45.00
☐ Pewter, lady's souvenir	30.00
☐ Pot metal	22.00
☐ Redware, lady's, 5″	38.00
☐ Silver plate, lady's, 7″	30.00
☐ Sterling silver, Gorham, 3½″	45.00
☐ White metal, man's, souvenir	22.00

SKULL

☐ Sitting on top of book	17.00

SQUARE

☐ Mother-of-pearl, velvet cushion	95.00
☐ Needlepoint in patchwork square, 8″	15.00
☐ Patchwork, 4″	5.00
☐ Red and white check squares alternate with black, hangs from ribbon, nineteenth century	40.00

STAR

☐ Beaded velvet, Victorian, 7¼″	30.00

STRAWBERRY

☐ Beaded satin, velvet top, 3″	35.00
☐ Velvet, sterling silver top, 3″	40.00

Pincushion. Lady's shoe, wood sole and heel painted brown, shoe painted black. Red, white and green beaded floral trim, satin ribbon bow, 4¾" long, $45.00.

CURRENT
PRICE

SWAN

☐ Pewter, 3½" 48.00

TABLE

☐ Oak, with one drawer, 4½" 40.00

TEDDY BEAR

☐ Fabric, tongue rolls out as tape measure, 7" ... 85.00

TOMATO

☐ Red satin 6.00
☐ Red satin, with green felt leaves, 5½"
diameter 22.00
☐ Red silk, with three babies climbing sides 18.00

Square pincushion. Needlepointed top with red velvet bottom, colorful squares, circa 1910, 3¼", $9.00.

CURRENT
PRICE

URN

☐ Cast iron, footed 17.00

VALISE

☐ Fabric, with sterling silver flap and handle 50.00

VEGETABLE

☐ Ivory and velvet 45.00

WOODEN SHOE

☐ Velvet cushion, 2½", Germany 9.00
☐ Velvet cushion, green and blue beading, 4" 15.00

YELLOW KID (Cartoon character)

☐ Silver metal, standing holding pincushion basket, wearing nightshirt 300.00

Pins

❀❀❀❀❀❀❀❀❀❀❀

A pin is any thin piece of metal that is tapered and sharp at one end and has a small knob at the other end. Pins, as is true with needles, have been used from very early times by all people. They were probably first used to simply hold garments together. Very wisely, small guards were also made to put over the points to protect the wearer.

Eventually, the pin began to evolve and it became a specialized tool. There has been a great increase in the types of pins made. They have been made for much more specific sewing purposes, in various metals and in various sizes: from very fine pins for work on silks and other fragile material, to dressmaker's pins, to household pins. But it did not end here; when very decorative knobs of worked metal, ivory, bone and jewels were added, the pins were used as accessories. Examples of these are hat pins, shawl pins and lace pins.

It is interesting to note that, originally, pins were very expensive and were very carefully kept in pin cases, or later in pincushions, so that they would not be lost. Since they were so expensive and difficult to obtain, they were

Paper fold with three rows of perforations to hold pins. Pins are no longer sold in this way; if you have one with the original pins, save it.

considered to be very acceptable and welcome presents. In fact, the expression "pin money," which is still in common use, is derived from those early days when a financial transaction for a merchant's wife was "for her pins."

For the most part, pins have not yet become a collectible. However, hat pins are in great demand. Other pins that are collected today are those found in their original holders. Most of these are recognized for the value of their advertising container.

Punches
(Stilettos)

🌼🌼🌼🌼🌼🌼🌼🌼🌼🌼

A punch, or stiletto, is a small, pointed instrument that was used to punch eyelet holes in fabric. Actually, although present-day terminology treats them as one, they are different tools. Punches have a more rounded point and are used to make embroidery eyelets. On the other hand, stilettos have a much sharper point and are used to make a belt eyelet. A stiletto is equivalent to an awl, which is the tool used in leather work or in any work requiring a heavy instrument.

Undoubtedly the most satisfactory and usable material for the manufacture of punches and stilettos is steel. However, they were also made of bone, ivory, silver and other metals.

Punches and stilettos are listed alphabetically by the material of which they were made.

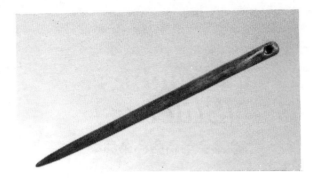

Punch. Bone, hand-carved, 7⅞″ long, $6.50.

CURRENT
PRICE

IVORY

☐ Plain 28.00
☐ Turnings on top, 3⅛″ 30.00
☐ Turnings on top, two punches, two sizes, in
    box 55.00

MOTHER-OF-PEARL

☐ Arrow-shaped handle, 1¾″ 22.00
☐ Carved handle, 4¼″, nineteenth century 65.00
☐ Plain, 2¾″ 10.00

SILVER, PLATE

☐ Embossed handle 12.00
☐ Plain 9.00

SILVER, STERLING

☐ Embossed floral handle 30.00
☐ Gauge in handle 35.00

Punch. Ivory with turned handle, 2⅞″ long, $30.00.

CURRENT
PRICE

STEEL

☐ Embossed handle 9.00
☐ Plain 8.00

Rulers

Seamstresses and needleworkers have always needed some way to measure their work. Whether measuring hems, seams, borders, the length of stitches, buttonhole widths, loop lengths or dress pieces, over the ages, many tools have been devised to accomplish this. Examples are hem gauges, knitting gauges and crochet gauges. Many of these tools performed dual or multi-purposes. Gauges or rulers have often been incorporated as a part of seam rippers, buttonhole cutters, hem gauges, knitting gauges, and crochet gauges (see Buttonhole Cutters and Gauges).

However, the most widely used tool to measure any work has been the simple ruler or yardstick. Early rulers were made of bone and ivory; later, in steel, wood and iron. No matter what they are made of, or when they were made, they all have either carved or printed demarcation in inches or meters.

During the late 1800s and into the 1900s, wood and metal rulers were popularly used as an advertising media. Today, many are found with advertisements for a great variety of

Rulers. *Top to bottom.* Advertising, local bank, black ink; advertising. "Exton's Celebrated Crackers," black ink; advertising for school supplies, multicolor; advertising for local shoe store, multicolor; plain in multicolor ink; $1.50–$2.00 each.

businesses, both national and local. The advertisements can be fascinating as well as valuable. But remember, advertisements for local concerns will have their greatest value in the immediate area of the business.

Rulers are listed alphabetically by the material of which they are made.

CURRENT
PRICE

EBONY

☐ With brass trim, 6″ 30.00
☐ With brass trim, 12″ 35.00

**CURRENT
PRICE**

IVORY

☐ Bound on ends with German silver 135.00
☐ Bound on ends with wood, four-fold 90.00
☐ Carved demarcations 150.00

METAL

☐ Painted black with silver demarcations, dou-
ble sides with slide in middle, 6″ 2.50

PLASTIC

☐ Keen Kutter, two-fold 12.50
☐ Prest-O-Lite, advertising, folding 10.00

STERLING SILVER

☐ Embossed demarcations, 4″ 50.00
☐ Embossed scroll work on handle, movable
marker, circa 1890s 75.00

WOOD

☐ Advertising, national product, 6″ 2.00
☐ Advertising, local business, yard stick 1.50
☐ Brass center and ends, 12″, tri-fold 10.00
☐ Brass center and ends, 24″, tri-fold 14.00
☐ Bound with ivory bands, four-fold 90.00
☐ Dressmaker's carved maple 27.00
☐ Hand-notched, eight panel sides, scribed
numbers 75.00
☐ Lufkin, brass ends, folding, 6″ 18.00
☐ Maple, merit award, Bible verse on reverse,
12″, 1920–present .... .75

Scissors

❧❧❧❧❧❧❧❧❧❧

There can hardly be a person alive who does not know what scissors are and what they do. A scissor consists of two sharp blades that are joined by either a pin or spring, and when brought together with a hand motion, has the ability to cut through certain materials. What is probably less known is that many different types of scissors have been manufactured over the years to perform very specific tasks. To perform these tasks scissors have always been made of very hardened materials such as cast iron, wrought iron, steel, silver and other metals. Often, particularly in small scissors, the handle was made of a different material than the blades. With the advent of household electricity, powered scissors were made. To this date, electric scissors have not stirred the interest of the collector.

There are many examples of scissors that are not related to sewing and needlework. More specifically, scissors used to perform personal grooming tasks have been made for centuries. Scissors such as these are used to cut cuticles, fingernails or eyebrows. Scissors to perform particular household tasks have also been made. For example, there are wick scissors (to trim candlewicks), grape scissors (to cut off grapes at the table) and egg cutting scissors (to halve the soft-boiled egg). Children's scissors with blunt, rounded ends have also been made. All of these scissors have been made in a variety of metals.

Needlework and sewing scissors generally fall into four categories. Embroidery scissors are small scissors with long, thin, sharp blades. Stork scissors are a specific type of embroidery scissors with figural stork handles in which the beak becomes the blade. Cutting out or trimming scissors generally have one straight blade and one rounded blade. Finally there are tailor's scissors or shears (large). Special shears have also been made, such as pinking shears. Scissors have also been made for left-handed people. These scissors have not yet gained any price advantage over their counterpart.

Buttonhole scissors, more commonly called buttonhole cutters, will be found under "Buttonhole Cutters."

Scissors are listed alphabetically by the type. Stork scissors are listed as a separate category. It should be noted that any antique or collectible scissor can be used today if the spring or pin mechanism is in working order, and if the blades are sharp or can be sharpened.

CURRENT
PRICE

EMBROIDERY SCISSORS

☐ Aluminum, advertising with figural shoe handles, "Star Brand Shoes are Better" 45.00

☐ Aluminum, political with portraits of McKinley and wife 40.00

☐ Brass, handles with embossed floral decoration, steel blades, circa 1850, 4″ 35.00

☐ Brass, handles with embossed decoration, steel blades, collapsible (handles fold into blades), 3½″ 35.00

☐ Gilt handles, nickeled blades, 3½″ 15.00

CURRENT
PRICE

☐ Gold-plated, marked "Toledo" on blades, 4″ ..   20.00
☐ Iron, marked "Edward Behr" 22.00
☐ Iron, figural handles, eighteenth century,
3¾″ 125.00
☐ Nickel-plated, Sears, Roebuck & Co., 4″ 10.00
☐ Silver plate, handles with Art Nouveau decoration, England, 4″ 18.00
☐ Silver plate, handles with embossed floral decoration, patent 1864, 3″ 20.00
☐ Steel, marked "Dixson Cutlery Co.,
Germany" 15.00
☐ Steel, marked "Griffin Cutlery Works, Germany," circa 1940, 4¼″ 7.00
☐ Steel, marked "H. Boh," nineteenth century ...   35.00
☐ Sterling silver, Germany, early 50.00
☐ Sterling silver, chased floral and scroll
decoration 55.00
☐ Sterling silver, engraved floral decoration 45.00
☐ Sterling silver, embossed handles, circa 1890,
4¼″ 60.00
☐ Sterling silver, embossed floral decoration on
handles, Germany 55.00
☐ Sterling silver, relief decoration on handles,
marked "Gorham" 35.00
☐ Sterling silver, circa 1900, 4¼″ 50.00

SHEARS AND CUTTERS

☐ Brass, Art Nouveau decorative handles 85.00
☐ Iron, hand-forged, eighteenth century, 12″ 95.00
☐ "Keen Kutter," 7″ 13.00
☐ "Keen Kutter," 7½″ 15.00
☐ Mother-of pearl handles, marked "E. Wisthof
Solingen" 65.00
☐ Nickel-plated blades, japanned bent handles,
circa 1904, 9″ 20.00

Scissors. Hand-wrought iron embroidery scissors, screw mechanism, marked "C.H. Beck," 3″ long, $25.00.

	CURRENT PRICE
☐ Nickel-plated blades, japanned bent handles, circa 1905, 10″	22.00
☐ Nickel-plated blades, japanned straight handles, circa 1910, 8″	15.00
☐ Nickel-plated, marked "Heinisch Straight Trimmers," circa 1910, 6″	15.00
☐ Universal, 12 tools in one	165.00
☐ "Winchester," 8″	32.00
☐ Wrought iron, eighteenth century, American ..	45.00

STORK-HANDLED SCISSORS

☐ Brass finish	25.00
☐ Silver and gold plate, 4″	30.00
☐ Silver plate, 3″	30.00
☐ Sterling silver	45.00
☐ Sterling silver in holder, Germany	60.00

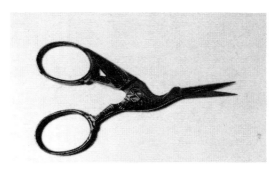

Scissors. Stork with feather detail on body, marked "Kru-sius/Germany/KBextra," 3⅝" long, $28.00.

TAILOR'S SHEARS

CURRENT
PRICE

- ☐ Brass joining, Patent 1859, 14" 65.00
- ☐ Iron, circa 1850–60s, 7½" 55.00
- ☐ Steel, japanned handles, bent trimmers, 10" .. 15.00
- ☐ Steel, japanned handles, marked "Heinisch,"
  12" 20.00
- ☐ Steel, japanned handles, marked "Heinisch,"
  sold by Sears, Roebuck & Co., specially made
  for upholsterers, carpet layers, and tailors,
  11¾" 25.00

Sewing Birds

✿✿✿✿✿✿✿✿✿✿✿

Sewing birds, also called hemming birds, were a type of sewing clamp. They conveniently had a bottom or side screw mechanism for attaching the bird to a piece of furniture. The bird, in figural form, is on the top and contains a spring or snap mechanism in the tail which, when pinched together, opens the bird's beak. The fabric being worked is placed in the beak to hold it tight. This is a very convenient item as it makes sewing faster and easier. Sewing birds are highly decorative and eagerly sought by collectors.

Early sewing birds were quite plain. However, from the middle of the nineteenth century into the early twentieth century, they were cast with highly elaborate floral decorations on the clamp and feathers and features on the bird were included. Pincushions could also be attached or incorporated into the design. Almost all sewing birds were cast in metal, brass, iron, silver or combinations of metals.

Sewing birds are listed alphabetically by the material of which they are made.

Sewing bird. Brass, double cushions of red velvet, embossed florals on bird and clamp, feather detail, $210.00.

	CURRENT PRICE

BRASS

☐ Double pincushions, embossed bird and clamp, patent September, 1853 .... 200.00

☐ Double pincushions, embossed bird and clamp 195.00

☐ Double pincushions, embossed bird and clamp, brass and silver plate 210.00

☐ No pincushion, embossed bird and clamp, 5¼″, thumbscrew in shape of a heart, brass and iron 175.00

☐ No pincushion, embossed bird and clamp, brass and silver plate 150.00

☐ No pincushion, embossed bird and clamp, 5″ 125.00

	CURRENT PRICE
☐ One pincushion, embossed bird and clamp, patent 1853, 5½″	120.00
☐ One pincushion, embossed bird and clamp, 5½″	120.00
☐ One pincushion, bird is a fat robin	225.00
☐ One pincushion in shape of a cocoon, bird is a robin	250.00
☐ One pincushion which forms the nest for the bird, embossed bird, clamp and nest	220.00
☐ One pincushion, patent 1853, brass and silver plate	130.00

BRONZE

☐ One pincushion, stamped floral and leaf decoration on clamp	95.00

IRON

☐ Double pincushion, late	60.00
☐ Double pincushion, gold lacquered. 5¼″, late	65.00
☐ No pincushion, 6″	90.00
☐ No pincushion, bird is a duck, clamp is for braiding rugs	185.00
☐ No pincushion, thumbscrew in shape of a heart, eighteenth century	280.00
☐ One pincushion, plain bird with a long sweeping curved tail which turns under	290.00
☐ One pincushion, 6½″	100.00
☐ One pincushion, plain bird. replaced pincushion	90.00

IVORY

☐ No pincushion, carved, very rare	425.00

CURRENT
PRICE

METAL

☐ Double pincushion, circa 1860 .... 130.00
☐ One pincushion, floral design on clamp 95.00

NICKEL-PLATED BRASS

☐ Double pincushion, embossed bird and clamp,
patent February, 1853 .... 175.00

SILVER, GERMAN

☐ One pincushion, embossed bird and clamp,
5½″ 90.00

SILVER, PLATED

☐ Double pincushion, embossed bird and clamp   165.00
☐ One pincushion, embossed bird and clamp 150.00
☐ One pincushion, embossed bird and clamp,
bird is a warbler, fitted to hold thimble 200.00

SILVER, STERLING

☐ No pincushion, plain bird, 6″ 265.00

STEEL

☐ No pincushion, embossed bird and clamp,
thumbscrew in shape of a heart, early 250.00
☐ One pincushion, bird has elongated "S"-
curved tail and rounded plain head, early
1800s 275.00

Sewing Clamps

❀❀❀❀❀❀❀❀❀❀

Sewing clamps are devices with some type of screw mechanism that can be firmly attached to a table, chair or shelf. The sewing clamp, in many cases, served two purposes. First, it held the material or fabric that was being worked with some degree of tension, thus making the sewing much easier and faster. Second, it often had, as an integral part of the clamp, fitted holders or drawers that provided convenient storage for objects used in sewing. Clamps were made with fitted holders for pincushions, pin and needle trays and/or drawers to hold thread and other sewing necessities. They were also fitted with candleholders and match boxes to provide convenient light. Sewing clamps have been made of wood, ivory, bone and metal. Naturally, the earliest ones were made of materials at hand.

Different sewing clamps were made for very specific sewing techniques. Clamps have been made for quilting, braiding rugs, netting and thread winding, to name a few. Today, probably the most collectible type of clamp is the sewing bird (also called a hemming bird). Sewing birds are listed in a separate category (see Sewing Birds).

Sewing clamps are listed alphabetically by the material of which they are made.

CURRENT
PRICE

BRASS

☐ With pincushion 40.00
☐ With pin tray, candleholder, and match
   holder 50.00

BRASS, PLATED OVER METAL

☐ Figural dog, scarce 235.00

IRON

☐ Hemming, swing arm 45.00
☐ Lyre shape, 4″ 175.00
☐ Quilting, set of 4 .... 50.00
☐ Swing arm, with open scroll work, 4½″ 45.00

IVORY

☐ Plain, with gauge, small 75.00

METAL

☐ Braiding rugs, under-table screw clamp, pres-
   sure bar on top 12.00
☐ Sewing machine shape top. "Singer," 7″ 55.00
☐ Victorian 55.00

WOOD

☐ Dovetailed drawer on top, walnut, 5″ x 6″ 325.00
☐ Round mirror and pincushion on top 95.00
☐ Shaker, cherry, table clamp with turned detail
   work 100.00

Sewing Machines

Until the invention of the domestic sewing machine, all sewing, dressmaking and embroidery had to be done by hand. It is very difficult for the modern-day seamstress to imagine the amount of time and patience it would take to make just one dress or to handmake just one sheet. The sewing machine saved hours of tedious work just by being able to do straight stitching. Our great grandmothers or grandmothers must have blessed the day that their first new "automatic" sewing machine came through the door.

A sewing machine is, in essence, simply a mechanism that combines the use of thread on a spool or bobbin, a needle and a source of power (hand crank, treadle, or electric) to produce a lock or chain stitch. At first they were used mainly for straight stitching or simple embroidery. As the sewing machines became more sophisticated, they could be used to produce very elaborate embroideries and other needlework techniques. The sewing machine also had a profound effect on dress styles, as much more trim and decorative touches could be added easily; hence, the emergence of more elaborate clothing styles during the 1870s–1890s.

The first domestic sewing machine was invented in 1825 by Barthelemy Thimonnier, a French tailor, who was engaged in the business of making uniforms for the French army. By 1831 he had 80 machines in full operation. As the story goes, this must have been seen as the modern equivalent of unfair trade practices by the other tailors and the sewing machines were destroyed. In 1845 Elias Howe of Boston, Massachusetts, invented the first really practical sewing machine. Improvements were made on these early machines by Isaac Singer, an American, who founded the Singer Corporation in 1864. After this date, the manufacture of sewing machines began in quantity by many manufacturers in America and Europe, and were priced so that most women could afford one. The Sears, Roebuck and Company catalog for 1902 lists a New Queen treadle sewing machine in a cabinet with four drawers for $10.45. Their best Minnesota sewing machine in a full, closing, very elaborate cabinet lists for $23.20.

The fact that many old sewing machines are still in use today and running as well as they ever did is a real tribute to the manufacturers of early sewing machines. Many sewers would not part with their reliable, old treadle machine. The cabinets that were made to hold the machine were also of a very high standard. They were solidly built (they had to hold the weight of the machine) and were often very elaborate. Unfortunately, many machines were lost when people bought them to use the cabinet as a piece of furniture, and discarded the sewing machine.

Other machines were also being made to produce lace, netting, knitting and weaving. However, these machines are not nearly as prevalent. Toy or children's sewing machines were made and were a favorite item to buy as a gift for little girls, because it was never too early for girls to begin to learn the art of sewing and needlework.

Sewing machines are listed alphabetically by manufacturer.

BURDICK

☐ Drop head, treadle, oak cabinet with two
drawers on each side, cast-iron base, circa
1900 .... 165.00

☐ Drop head, treadle, oak cabinet with five
drawers, cast-iron base, circa 1900 .... 170.00

☐ Drop head, treadle, oak cabinet with swinging,
fitted full door, circa 1900 .... 245.00

☐ High arm, treadle, drop leaf walnut cabinet
with seven drawers, cast-iron base, circa
1900 .... 195.00

BUSY BEE

☐ Hand crank, cast iron, New England, 3¼" x
6" base 75.00

ELDRIDGE, B.

☐ Hand crank, full size, for Wanamaker, circa
1880 .... 85.00

FRANZ AND POPE KNITTING MACHINE CO.

☐ Hand crank, cast iron with original black
paint, red and yellow striping, original embossed metal label, patent 1872, 10" long 40.00

HOWE, ELIAS

☐ Treadle, cast-iron base, patent 1871 .... 225.00

GERMANY

☐ Child's, red painted tin, 7" 25.00

CURRENT
PRICE

GATEWAY

☐ Child's, lithographed tin 45.00

MINNESOTA

☐ Drop head, treadle, full oak cabinet with drop
leaf and two swing-in doors. 220.00
☐ Drop head, with automatic drop desk cabinet,
treadle veneer trim on solid walnut cabinet,
two swing-in doors. 295.00

NEW HOME

☐ Drop head, treadle, oak cabinet with three
drawers on each side, cast-iron base, circa
1879 .... 170.00

NEW QUEEN

☐ Drop head, treadle, oak cabinet with two
drawers on each side, cast-iron base with
Sears, Roebuck logo on treadle and supports,
circa 1900 .... 165.00

NEW WANZER

☐ Treadle, patent 1882, with original instruc-
tions and parts list 125.00

REMINGTON

☐ Full size, portable, patent 1879 .... 145.00

ROYAL ST. JOHN

☐ Drop head, ebonized case with three drawers
on each side 175.00

New Home treadle sewing machine. Oak cabinet, cast-iron
supports, Model SMOO, Orange, MA, Pat. 2, 1887, $170.00.

	CURRENT PRICE

SINGER

☐ Child's, original box, 1955 .... 55.00
☐ Child's, Singer logo on machine, no box 38.00
☐ Drop head, treadle, oak cabinet with drawers,
   ornate cast-iron base, gold stenciled logo on
   machine 255.00
☐ Drop head, treadle, oak cabinet with six draw-
   ers, cast-iron base 250.00
☐ Heavy duty 175.00
☐ Hemstitcher 85.00
☐ Machine only, cast iron, painted black with
   gold stenciling 75.00

Singer electric portable. Walnut wood carrying case, circa 1900, working condition, $95.00.

	CURRENT PRICE
☐ Model 29K71	185.00
☐ Portable, electric, oak case with gold stenciling	80.00
☐ Table model, treadle, patent 1876	125.00
☐ Traveling, Singer logo, 6″	40.00

SMITH AND EGGE

☐ Child's, "Little Comfort Improved," cast iron with chrome fittings, original paint, patent 1897, 7″ x 7″	150.00
☐ Hand crank, "Improved"	145.00
☐ Hand crank, fitted with table clamp and needle holder, patent 1901	125.00

UNKNOWN MAKERS

☐ Drop head, treadle, oak cabinet, cast-iron base, complete with attachment box, patent 1889	155.00

CURRENT
PRICE

☐ Table, cast iron with original black paint, claw
feet, nineteenth century, 11″ x 7″ x 9″ 55.00

VICTOR

☐ Drop head, treadle, walnut cabinet, patent
1875 ....   195.00

WHEELER & WILSON

☐ Drop head, originally treadle and has been
electrified, oak cabinet, cast-iron base 145.00

WHITE

☐ Drop head, treadle, oak cabinet, cast-iron
base, early 1900s 165.00

WILCOX & GIBBS

☐ Gooseneck head, treadle, walnut cabinet, circa
1880s 195.00
☐ Lap, hand crank, patent April 17, 1883 ....   145.00
☐ Model 1502, patent 1882 ....   160.00
☐ Table, hand crank, clamp on, patent 1871 ......   130.00

Shuttles

There are two distinctly different types of shuttles used in sewing and needlework. The first type is the metal boat or round-shaped case, which holds the threaded metal bobbin and is placed in the sewing machine. It has a mechanism that allows the bottom thread to be fed out easily and with an adjustable amount of tension in machine stitching. This type of shuttle is not considered a collectible—yet.

The second type of shuttle is simply a tool on which the thread can be wound and then easily unwound as needed. In this sense a thread winder (see Thread Winders) or an ordinary spool is a shuttle. Bobbins are also, under this definition, a shuttle. However, ordinarily the term shuttle implies an implement used in tatting, knotting or netting. Tatting, knotting and netting shuttles have been made in wood, ivory, metals and bone. Early ones were made of materials at hand, with later shuttles being made in silver or in other more decorative ways.

Shuttles have also been used in weaving and in industrial manufacture of fabrics. This type of shuttle includes the

Shuttles, industrial. *Left.* Light wood with metal rims on ends, 4³/₄″ long, $2.50. *Middle.* Weaving shuttle, mixed woods, 16″ long, $16.00. *Right.* Light wood with metal rims on ends, 7¹/₈″ long, $4.00.

various-sized wood spools and the barge-shaped weaving shuttles.

Shuttles are listed alphabetically by the material of which they are made.

CURRENT
PRICE

BONE

☐ Tatting, plain, 2½″ 10.00

CELLULOID

☐ Tatting, plain, black 4.00
☐ Tatting, cream, pair 10.00
☐ Tatting, plain, white 4.00

IVORINE

☐ Tatting, plain 5.00

Shuttles. *Top.* Red and natural marble pattern celluloid, 3⅛", $4.00. *Bottom.* Black plastic, 3¼", $ .75.

CURRENT
PRICE

IVORY

☐ Tatting, carved with scenes of people 55.00
☐ Tatting, carved few geometric lines 40.00
☐ Tatting, plain, nineteenth century 34.00

METAL

☐ Tatting, bobbin on one end, flat hook on other
    end, 1923 ....   24.00
☐ Tatting, Lydia Pinkham advertising 15.00
☐ Tatting, Lydia Pinkham advertising, attached
    needle and thread case 45.00
☐ Tatting, plain 4.50

SILVER, GERMAN

☐ Tatting, plain 12.00

Shuttles. *Left.* Ivory, 1³/₄″ long, $18.00. *Middle.* Wood with turned knob ends, 1¹/₄″ long, $3.50. *Right.* Wood with turned knob ends, 1¹/₄″, $3.50.

	CURRENT PRICE
SILVER, STERLING	
☐ Tatting, embossed floral decoration	38.00
☐ Tatting, embossed ornate medallion decoration	40.00
☐ Tatting, plain	30.00
TORTOISE SHELL	
☐ Tatting, plain	24.00

WHALE BONE

☐ Lace, scrimshaw, handle with ring of Venetian
  beads at top for decoration, circa 1870s 60.00
☐ Plain, 1¼″ 18.00

WHALE IVORY

☐ Plain, 2¾″ 85.00

WOOD

☐ Netting, plain, 11″ 22.00
☐ Tatting, plain, 3″, early 45.00

Spinning Wheels

❀❀❀❀❀❀❀❀❀❀

For our ancestors, producing fabric was a long, very time-consuming process, and many tools had to be used. One very important implement found in most homes was the spinning wheel. It was used after the wool or flax had gone through many stages and was finally made into fibers. Now it could be placed on the distaff of the spinning wheel to be processed into yarn. The larger spinning wheel was used to spin wool, while the small wheel was used to spin flax. Since the small flax wheels were easier to store and move, they are more commonly found today. However, be aware that very often these spinning wheels are missing the distaff or other parts.

Most spinning wheels were quite plain with very little decoration. However, some have quite elaborate wood or other inlays. Also, many of the spinning wheels from Scandinavia and certain areas in Canada were found to be painted. As imagined, these can be very beautiful pieces.

Spinning wheels are listed alphabetically by the wood of which they are made.

Spinning Wheel. Wool wheel, mixed woods with all parts intact, working condition, circa early eighteenth century, $650.00.

CURRENT
PRICE

MAHOGANY

☐ Flax wheel, bone parts, 32″ wheel, English,
   circa 1850s 375.00

☐ Flax wheel, enamel inlays, turned ivory finial
   ring with brass bells, 34″ wheel 175.00

MAPLE

☐ Flax wheel, New England, circa 1830 .... 275.00

CURRENT
PRICE

MIXED WOODS

☐ Flax wheel, child's, 22″ wheel	285.00
☐ Flax wheel, fruitwood and oak, 36″ wheel, American, circa 1830s	250.00
☐ Flax wheel, hickory and ash, carved detail on block, pine bobbin box, 30¾″ wheel	250.00
☐ Flax wheel, Pennsylvania, turned detail, circa 1840, 32″ wheel	300.00
☐ Flax wheel, Pennsylvania, turned detail, incised heart decoration, circa 1810	475.00
☐ Flax wheel, Samuel Ring	450.00
☐ Flax wheel, Shaker, all complete	575.00
☐ Upright, iron parts, wood bobbin and treadle, 29″ wheel	190.00
☐ Wool wheel, 45″ wheel	235.00
☐ Wool wheel, turned detail, circa 1840	400.00

OAK

☐ Wool walking wheel, plain, 45″ wheel	275.00
☐ Wool walking wheel, cast-iron parts, 30″ wheel	300.00
☐ Wool walking wheel, turned legs, posts, spindles, 44½″ wheel	250.00

PAINTED

☐ Norwegian, painted decoration, small	225.00
☐ Flax wheel, worn blue paint	200.00

WALNUT

☐ Wool wheel, Pennsylvania, circa 1850s	450.00
☐ Wool walking wheel, Pennsylvania, circa 1850s	450.00

Store Cabinets

❀❀❀❀❀❀❀❀❀❀

Most store cabinets were produced from the middle of the nineteenth century and into the twentieth century. They were found in the general store displaying thread, needles, shuttles, braid and embroidery floss. With partitions to keep the various material sorted by size and color, they were also a convenient display of advertising for various manufacturers. Generally they were made of wood, but a few could probably be found of tin.

Store cabinets have been eagerly sought by collectors. They are aesthetically pleasing and make an ideal display and storage space for small collectibles. They are also collected for their advertising value.

Store cabinets are listed alphabetically by the advertising manufacturer.

Store cabinet. No advertising, walnut needle cabinet with 15 divisions in each drawer with original labels for needle sizes, 15¾" long × 7⅜" wide × 6⅝" high, $195.00.

CURRENT
PRICE

A. A. CO.

☐ Two-drawer, pine, braid cabinet 125.00

BELDING BROS.

☐ Two-drawer, spool silk cabinet, small 85.00
☐ Thirteen-drawer, spool silk cabinet, 34" high . 485.00

BROOKS

☐ Four-drawer 350.00

BOYE

☐ One-drawer, wooden base, needle cabinet 150.00

☐ Revolving counter cabinet for shuttles and
bobbins, 1929 .... 165.00

CLARK'S O.N.T. THREAD

☐ Two-drawer, ruby glass panels 225.00
☐ Two-drawer, walnut 175.00
☐ Three-drawer, ruby glass panels 375.00
☐ Four-drawer, desk style, oak, 30" 435.00
☐ Six-drawer, brass handles 800.00
☐ Six-drawer, hinged top 510.00

COATS, J. P., THREAD

☐ Two-drawer, tin front, oak 150.00
☐ Four-drawer 350.00
☐ Four-drawer, leather lift top, inset for inkwell,
oak 395.00
☐ Six-drawer, slanted desk top 650.00
☐ Six-drawer, cherry 575.00
☐ Slanted desk top, oak 485.00
☐ Slanted desk top, hinged lid, small 95.00
☐ Top lift, swivel base, sides roll up 425.00

CORTICELLI

☐ Five-drawer 435.00
☐ Twelve-drawer, one glass drawer 525.00

CRAWLEY'S

☐ Needle cabinet 95.00

DEXTER FINE YARN

☐ Four-drawer, oak, 18¾" × 17⅛" 560.00

EUREKA

☐ Twenty-two drawers, sixteen with glass 850.00

GEM PERRY & CO.

☐ Six-part, hinged cover, London, needle
cabinet 155.00

GOFF'S BEST BRAID

☐ Three-drawers, melon-shaped pulls 315.00

HEMINGWAY SILKS

☐ Three-drawer, revolving, oak 375.00

LILY

☐ Metal 45.00

MERRICK

☐ Two large drawers over two small drawers 375.00
☐ Double drum, revolving dispenser, four curved
glass panels, oak 900.00
☐ Mirrored sides, 1897 .... 580.00
☐ Revolving center dispenser, two glass panels,
20″ 350.00
☐ Rounded ends, mirrored sides 575.00

RICHARDSON'S SPOOL SILK

☐ Two drawers 235.00

STAR TWIST THREAD

☐ Thirty compartments, glass front 80.00

WILLARDS

☐ Two-drawer, oak, 13¼″ × 8¼″ 185.00

Store cabinet. Willimantic Silk Thread, walnut, original decals on front and sides, wood pulls, 13″ high × 24¾″ wide (base and legs added), $450.00.

CURRENT
PRICE

WILLIMANTIC

☐ Two drawers, original pulls 190.00

NO ADVERTISING

☐ Portable, folding legs, two doors, ten spool
holders, 14″ × 17″ 200.00
☐ Two-drawer, original pulls, oak 190.00
☐ Two-drawer, walnut 185.00
☐ Six-drawer, walnut with red glass panels 600.00

	CURRENT PRICE
☐ Nine-drawer, oak, 24″ × 21″ × 17″	750.00
☐ Braid cabinet, three drawers, 24″ × 17″, oak	325.00
☐ Desk top, six-drawer, oak, 33″ × 23″ × 17″	450.00

Sunbonnet Babies

❀❀❀❀❀❀❀❀❀❀

The little children known as the Sunbonnet Babies were created in the very early 1900s by Bertha Louise Corbett, an accomplished artist. Legend has it that Bertha Corbett did not feel that she was competent at drawing faces, and therefore all the little babies' faces were completely hidden by large sunbonnets. The Sunbonnet Babies were depicted doing many things. Household chores were a frequent motif: cleaning, washing, sweeping, ironing, sewing, mending, cooking and baking. Other activities were reading, playing, fishing, playing with small animals or toys, to name a few.

The earliest appearances of the Sunbonnet Babies in color were as illustrations in the "Sunbonnet Babies Primer." They immediately became very popular and began to appear on all types of items including children's China dishes, door stops, bookends, bookmarks, greeting cards and postcards. Royal Bayreuth of Bavaria produced a full line of children's dishes decorated with the Sunbonnet Babies, and these items

Sunbonnet Babies. Quilt square, red embroidery on natural linen, $10.00.

are undoubtedly the most expensive form of the Babies memorabilia.

Of particular interest for the sewing and needlework collector is the wide range of household linens that were generally appliqued and/or embroidered with Sunbonnet Baby designs. Towels, pillowcases, pillow shams, dresser and table scarfs, quilts, and blankets all were avidly worked. Luckily, old patterns and early embroidery transfers can still be found. However, the greatest discovery for the needlework collector would be a sewing box, pinbox, figural pincushion or thimble stand decorated with the figures engaged in sewing or mending.

Sunbonnet Babies are listed alphabetically by the type of item with the exception that Royal Bayreuth is listed separately.

CURRENT
PRICE

BELL

☐ Royal Bayreuth, Sunbonnet Babies washing
   clothes 340.00

CURRENT
PRICE

BOOKENDS

☐ Cast iron, pair 75.00

BOOKS

☐ ABC, 1935 edition 55.00
☐ "Sunbonnet Babies in Mother Goose Land,"
 1934 edition 60.00

BOX

☐ Wood, Sunbonnet Babies playing with kittens
 decal on lid, circa 1940s 20.00
☐ Wood, Sunbonnet Babies wood burned on lid,
 circa 1940s 25.00

CALENDAR

☐ 1908, top with litho of Sunbonnet Babies play-
 ing, all complete 22.00

CARDS

☐ Birthday card, Tuck, Sunbonnet Babies
 playing 5.00
☐ General greeting card, Sunbonnet Baby sitting
 with doll 4.00
☐ Valentine, Tuck 4.50

CHINA—ALL ROYAL BAYREUTH CHINA

☐ Bowl, 5″, footed, Sunbonnet Babies with
 sled 90.00
☐ Bowl, 7½″, Sunbonnet Babies cleaning 350.00
☐ Bowl, cereal, Sunbonnet Babies fishing 125.00
☐ Candlestick, with handle and hood, Sunbon-
 net Babies cleaning 250.00

	CURRENT PRICE
☐ Candlestick, Sunbonnet Babies sweeping	225.00
☐ Creamer, 3½″, Sunbonnet Babies ironing	225.00
☐ Creamer, 3½″, Sunbonnet Babies mending	235.00
☐ Cup and saucer, Sunbonnet Babies ironing	180.00
☐ Cup and saucer, demitasse	110.00
☐ Mug, blue mark	125.00
☐ Nappy, Sunbonnet Babies sweeping	145.00
☐ Pitcher, Sunbonnet Babies washing and ironing	225.00
☐ Plate, 6″, Sunbonnet Babies sewing	100.00
☐ Plate, 6½″, Sunbonnet Babies ironing	100.00
☐ Plate, 7½″, Sunbonnet Babies fishing	125.00
☐ Sugar bowl, Sunbonnet Babies washing clothes	110.00
☐ Sugar bowl, Sunbonnet Babies fishing	125.00

CHINA—OTHER MANUFACTURERS

☐ Candlesticks, Sunbonnet Babies mending, unmarked, pair	145.00
☐ Cereal set, cup, bowl and plate, unmarked	45.00
☐ Creamer, Sunbonnet Babies mending	45.00
☐ Cup and saucer, demitasse, Germany	50.00
☐ Cup and saucer, Sunbonnet Babies cutting, stitching and sewing, Germany	65.00
☐ Plate, 6″, Sunbonnet Babies carrying kittens, unmarked, probably Germany	90.00
☐ Plate, 8½″, Sunbonnet Babies mending, unmarked	95.00
☐ Platter, 10½″, Sunbonnet Babies washing and ironing, unmarked	85.00

DOORSTOP

☐ Cast iron, 6″	65.00

FIGURINE

☐ Cast iron, 6″, painted 45.00

LINENS

☐ Doll blanket, embroidered in red, Sunbonnet
Babies doing various activities 45.00
☐ Dresser scarf, 24″ long, embroidered 24.00
☐ Pillow cover, embroidered and appliqued, very
colorful 22.00
☐ Quilt, crib size, ten blocks embroidered in red,
red embroidery joins 135.00
☐ Quilt, single bed size, appliqued, very colorful 150.00
☐ Quilt, double bed size, appliqued and embroi-
dered, blue and white 250.00
☐ Towels, linen, set of seven, "Days of the
Week," embroidered 45.00
☐ Towel, linen, hand, Sunbonnet Babies
washing 10.00

NEEDLE CASE

☐ Figural, green felt and green ribbon, 4″ 11.00

POSTCARDS

☐ Advertising 8.00–
12.00
☐ Set of seven, "Days of the Week," each 12.00
☐ Set of six, motto series 60.00

PRINTS

☐ Bertha Corbett, signed and framed 40.00–
50.00

CURRENT
PRICE

RATTLE

☐ Celluloid, figural 35.00

TITLES, CERAMIC

☐ Sunbonnet Babies, sewing 18.00
☐ Sunbonnet Babies, ironing 18.00

WALL PLAQUE

☐ Brass, Sunbonnet Babies ironing 25.00

Sunbonnet Babies. Crib quilt, very unusual pattern, red embroidery on white background, all hand-sewn and quilted, heart quilting in white squares, $275.00.

Tape Measures

❀❀❀❀❀❀❀❀❀❀

At the present time, tape measures are strictly utilitarian. They are lengths of white or colored nylon, polyester or pliable plastic that are marked off in a contrasting color in units of inches or centimeters. However, during the eighteenth and nineteenth centuries, they were made in many very interesting, decorative and whimsical figural forms. The forms included most of the figures that were popularly depicted during these times including children, men, women, animals, hats; the list is lengthy. These figures could be made of wood, metal, ivory, porcelain, or celluloid. The tape measures were generally made of silk or linen. Early figural tape measures contained a wire pin upon which the tape could be wound. The figural form then had an exterior knob incorporated into the design for rewinding the tape. Later, spring devices were used in the interior of the form for automatic rewinding. These tape measures are very lovely and are fun additions to the sewing basket.

Although tape measures, as we know them, are marked

in inches or centimeters, this was not always the case. Prior to 1850, they were often marked in nails:

N (nail) = 2¼"
HQ (half quarter) = 4½"
Q (quarter) = 9"
H (half yard) = 18"
Y (yard) = 36"

In the late 1800s and into the 1900s many tape measures were made as advertising giveaways. These were made of celluloid, wood or plastic and were generally round objects with the tape measure coiled inside loaded on a spring. The product or company was advertised on the top. These have become very collectible, and, of course, the tape measures that advertise certain products, such as railroads or telephones, draw the interest of collectors in those specific fields. Tape measures that depict figures, such as animals, will also appeal to the collector.

Tape measures were also made to commemorate certain events. It is not uncommon to find souvenir tape measures of world, state and local fairs, expositions and the anniversaries of specific events. Souvenir tape measures were also made depicting popular tourist spots. Why not start your collection on your next trip?

Tape measures are listed alphabetically by the shape in which they were made, with the exception that advertising and commemorative tape measures are listed separately.

CURRENT
PRICE

ADVERTISING AND COMMEMORATIVE

☐ Abbot's Ice Cream, lithograph of milkmaid and pail, celluloid	11.00
☐ American Telephone	10.00
☐ Aunt Jemima	5.00
☐ B & M Station, Winnisquam, New Hampshire, celluloid	21.00
☐ Baby Ruth	48.00

Tape measure. Figural wood bell, black decal of Longfellow Home, Portland, ME, linen tape, top wind tape mechanism, 2″ high, 1⅜″ diameter at base, $45.00.

	CURRENT PRICE
☐ Bliss Native Herbs	4.00
☐ Central Mutual Insurance Co.	13.00
☐ Chicago Electric Show, celluloid, 1919	17.00
☐ Cologate, Fab, picture of soap box	18.50
☐ Converse Bridge Company, celluloid	8.00
☐ Curtis & Spindell Company, elastic stockings, aluminum	9.00
☐ Dixie Lye	14.00
☐ Edwardian woman, lithograph, circa 1900	14.00
☐ Emaus National Bank, "A Measure of Appreciation from the Emaus National Bank," Emaus, Pennsylvania, 1½″	25.00
☐ G.E. Refrigerators, celluloid	18.00
☐ Hawk Work Clothes, picture of hawk	19.00
☐ Hoover Vacuum Cleaners, figural vacuum cleaner	28.00
☐ Illinois Surgical Supply Co.	27.00
☐ John Deere Tractor	24.00

	CURRENT PRICE
☐ Kansas City Life Insurance	18.00
☐ Lewis Lye, celluloid	12.00
☐ Lydia Pinkham, celluloid	39.00
☐ Mark Twain Shirts, celluloid	15.00
☐ Morrell Meats, plastic	10.00
☐ Morrell, John, Meats, celluloid	12.00
☐ Mountain States Rubber	10.00
☐ Mr. Peanut	8.00
☐ Mr. Peanut, boxed	10.00
☐ New York World's Fair, 1939, celluloid	9.00
☐ Oldsmobile	14.00
☐ Phelphs & Armstead Furniture	24.00
☐ Pennsylvania Central Railroad	30.00
☐ Phoenix Beer, "Buffalo's Famous Brew"	14.00
☐ Rainbow Trove, St. Johnsbury, Vermont, 4½"	32.00
☐ Sear's, Roebuck & Company, plows	38.00
☐ Silk Floss Mattresses, Boston, celluloid	39.00
☐ Singer, "Century of Sewing Progress, 1851–1951"	28.00
☐ Spring Valley, Wisconsin, celluloid	9.00
☐ Star Brand Shoes, celluloid	11.00
☐ Straw hat, figural, "Most Hats Cover the Head, This Covers the Feet"	55.00
☐ Taylor Trousers, Newton, Iowa, metal	12.00
☐ Tartanware	55.00
☐ Tension Saddlery, Dallas, Texas, celluloid	22.00
☐ Tire, figural, "Radial Ride by Riverside"	28.00
☐ Trojan Ice Cream	7.00
☐ Waukewam Lake, Meredith, New Jersey	15.00
☐ Whitehead Metal, tin	8.00

ALARM CLOCK

☐ Hands turn when tape is pulled	65.00
☐ Large bell, footed	32.00

ALLIGATOR
☐ Pink, green, black, celluloid 21.00

APPLE
☐ Red, celluloid 24.00

AUNT JEMIMA
☐ Tape measure rolls out from skirt, 4½″,
    celluloid 48.00

BANJO
☐ Celluloid 45.00

BARREL
☐ Native on side, celluloid 70.00

BASKET OF FLOWERS
☐ Celluloid 43.00
☐ Plastic, circa 1950 .... 6.00

BASKET OF FRUIT
☐ Celluloid 37.00

BEAR
☐ Celluloid 35.00

BEEHIVE
☐ Wood, wind up tape, circa 1860s 220.00

BLACK MAMMY
☐ Full figure, ladybug tape pull, celluloid 48.00

CURRENT
PRICE

BLACK MAN

☐ Celluloid 115.00

BOOK

☐ Leather, gold-tooled, 1³/₄″, Austria 26.00

BOTTLE

☐ Whiskey, stopper is pull out tape, marked
"Kentucky" 20.00

BOY

☐ Porcelain, 4″, Germany 95.00

BUTTERFLY

☐ Celluloid 45.00
☐ Celluloid, 1¹/₄″, Germany 40.00

CAT

☐ Brass, head only, glass eyes, 1¹/₂″ 48.00
☐ Celluloid, 2¹/₂″, Occupied Japan 20.00
☐ With dog, white metal 65.00

CHALET

☐ Wood, 1800s 195.00

CHAMPAGNE BOTTLE IN COOLER

☐ Wood, windup, 1800s 185.00

CHICKEN

☐ Brass, worn in mouth turns and pulls out 215.00

CURRENT
PRICE

CLAM SHELL

☐ Metal 7.00

CLOCK

☐ Carriage, brass and celluloid 60.00
☐ Enamel and metal, tape pulls out from side,
   top handle 45.00
☐ Mantel, brass footed 42.00
☐ Works 65.00

CLOWN

☐ China 35.00
☐ Head with hat 95.00

COCKATOO

☐ White metal, 1800s 225.00

CORONATION COACH

☐ With red windows 45.00

CYLINDER

☐ Ivory, Stanhope, view of Eiffel Tower 55.00
☐ Ivory, Stanhope finial, painted 45.00

DOG

☐ Cast iron, bulldog 22.00
☐ Celluloid, wearing captain's hat, holding bin-
   oculars, white 85.00
☐ Fur, black, tail pulls out, 1½″ 60.00
☐ Metal, head, wearing hat, kerchief, tongue
   pulls out 35.00

☐ Plush, tongue pulls out with tape, tail is thimble holder, 4″ × 4½″ 20.00
☐ Scotty, sitting on tree stump, circa 1930, Japan 25.00
☐ Scotty, sitting on pincushion base 42.00
☐ Velour, standing, red plastic collar, tongue pulls out with tape, tail is thimble holder, 4¾″ × 4¾″ 35.00

DUCK AND HEN

☐ Celluloid 35.00

DUTCH GIRL

☐ Pottery, tape measure in base 22.00

EGG

☐ Glass, plain pull 9.00
☐ Tin, fly pull sitting on top 330.00

ELEPHANT

☐ Bone 45.00
☐ Cast clay 52.00
☐ Celluloid 34.00
☐ Fabric 40.00
☐ Plastic 25.00

FISHING REEL

☐ Wood and brass 80.00

FLASK

☐ Sterling silver 55.00

FOOTSTOOL

☐ Wood 27.00

FRENCH GIRL
☐ Celluloid 45.00

FRUIT
☐ Celluloid 35.00

GIRL
☐ Porcelain, with mandolin 38.00

GLOBE
☐ World, thimble holder on top, base holds tape
measure 35.00

HARLEQUIN WOMAN
☐ Porcelain, Occupied Japan 45.00

HEAD
☐ Porcelain, English butler, fly sits on head and
pulls out tape 85.00

HELMET
☐ Spike on top pulls out tape 125.00

HORSE
☐ Celluloid, red painted saddle, Japan 18.00

KANGAROO
☐ Celluloid, baby in pouch 45.00
☐ Wood, baby in pouch, windup, circa 1830 ...... 250.00

MALTESE CROSS

☐ Porcelain, 1914 .... 80.00

MONKEY

☐ Brass, windup, circa 1800s 250.00
☐ Fabric, stuffed pincushion 25.00

OWL

☐ Brass, embossed face 30.00
☐ Brass, sitting on limb, glass eyes 32.00
☐ Celluloid 25.00
☐ Metal, glass eyes 26.00

PADDLE WHEEL BOAT

☐ Brass, circa 1830 .... 80.00

PAPOOSE

☐ Fabric, original box 21.00

PENGUIN

☐ Celluloid, blue, pink and white, Occupied
Japan 36.00

PIG

☐ Brass 45.00
☐ Brass, tail turns to pull out tape 95.00
☐ Brass, nickeled, marked "Niagara Falls" 70.00
☐ Celluloid 22.00
☐ Celluloid, standing, Occupied Japan 40.00
☐ Metal, silvered, 1800s 125.00

POLICEMAN

☐ Celluloid, gun pulls tape measure 45.00

CURRENT
PRICE

PUPPY

☐ Fabric, plaid, tail pulls tape measure 27.00

PYRAMID

☐ Metal, gold-colored, girl inset 36.00

RABBIT

☐ Celluloid 45.00
☐ Fabric 22.00
☐ With wheelbarrow, windup, circa 1860s 220.00

RIP VAN WINKLE

☐ Celluloid 50.00

ROOSTER

☐ Tape pulls out of mouth, sits on pin tray 12.00

ROUND

☐ Aluminum, impressed floral spray design, 3″ . 10.00
☐ Bone, with ivory knob, pink tape 46.00
☐ Celluloid, inscribed American flags, Liberty
   Bell, "1776–1926" 65.00
☐ Celluloid, impressed rose design 45.00
☐ Girl in full color, long dark hair, green cap,
   1″, Germany 11.00
☐ Girl in multicolor lithograph holding flowers,
   1½″ 48.00
☐ Ivory, cloth tape measure, circa 1750, 3″ 85.00
☐ Metal, impressed sunflower design 15.00
☐ Metal, impressed kittens playing 24.00
☐ Sterling silver, embossed face design, 1½″ 65.00
☐ Sterling silver, embossed Greek Key design 60.00
☐ Sterling silver, embossed holly design 65.00
☐ Walnut 40.00

Tape measure. *Left.* Chrome case, spring-load return, linen tape, 1⁷/₁₆″ diameter, $8.00. *Right.* White metal case with engraved and embossed floral design, spring-load return, 1⁷/₁₆″ diameter, $6.50.

CURRENT
PRICE

SAD IRON

☐ Cast iron, 3″ 38.00

SHIPS, SAILING

☐ Celluloid 90.00
☐ Ivorine 45.00

SHOE

☐ Brass, man's work shoe, "Three feet in one
  shoe" 45.00
☐ Silver plate, man's work shoe, "Three feet in
  one shoe" 50.00
☐ With pincushion, 1800s 190.00

SQUIRREL

☐ Celluloid 35.00

CURRENT
PRICE

STRAW HAT

☐ Embossed on top, "Most Hats Cover the Head,
This Covers the Feet" 55.00

TEA KETTLE

☐ Brass 65.00
☐ Copper, 2¼″ 75.00

TEDDY BEAR

☐ Fabric, stuffed, 3″ 45.00

TOP

☐ Ivory, spinning 50.00

TOWER

☐ Ivory, pincushion on top, 3″ 110.00

TURTLE

☐ Silver plate, "Pull My Head" 45.00
☐ Sterling silver, brass and enamel 85.00
☐ Sterling silver 100.00

VAULT

☐ Celluloid 35.00

VICTORIAN HOUSE

☐ Celluloid 47.00

WINDMILL

☐ Brass 55.00

CURRENT
PRICE

WOMAN

☐ Celluloid, wearing hoop skirt, Germany 60.00
☐ China, Germany 45.00

Thimble Cases

❀❀❀❀❀❀❀❀❀❀

Although thimbles have been a useful tool in sewing and needlework since the craft began, the history of the thimble case is much more recent. It wasn't until thimbles became more elaborate, often made of precious metals and jewels, that small cases were also needed. A decorated thimble in its case was a welcomed gift that was highly valued. Undoubtedly, these thimbles were only used on special occasions and were otherwise kept carefully in their own case.

Thimble cases were small, for they were made to hold just one thimble. They were made of many materials, bone, ivory, metals, wood, and woven sweet grass, to name a few. Most often the thimble and the case were made of the same material, but obviously this was not always true. For the collector, the greatest find in thimble cases is one which contains the original thimble; unfortunately, this is sometimes difficult to determine.

Thimble cases are listed alphabetically by the material of which they were made. Thimble case prices are for the case only unless otherwise noted.

Thimble case. Woven sweet grass, $5.50 without thimble.

CURRENT
PRICE

BAMBOO

☐ Acorn shape, slip over top, highly polished 60.00

BONE

☐ Carved, with straight lines, slip over top 45.00

BLACKTHORN

☐ Carved, with harp and shamrock design on
top and sides, slip over top, Ireland 40.00

BRASS

☐ Egg shape, engraved in floral design, with
brass chain, hinged top 55.00

☐ Mesh body, embossed decoration at ends, jewels in clasp, modern 28.00

☐ Mother-of-pearl and gold insets, in grapes and leaf design, hinged 120.00

CHINA

☐ Floral, hand-painted design, hinged, unmarked 35.00

CROCHET

☐ Basket shape, with handle and cover 20.00

ENAMEL

☐ Yellow enamel over a guilloche, hinged, thimble with carnelian top 185.00

IVORY

☐ Barrel shape, with horizontal carved lines, 1½″ 55.00

☐ Round with thimble top, circa 1800s 75.00

☐ Vegetable shape, no carving 35.00

LEATHER

☐ Gold decoration in scroll and feather design 80.00

☐ Plain, lined in blue velvet and silk, gilded fastener 25.00

☐ Plain, South Africa 22.00

MAUCHLINE

☐ Egg shape, plain, slip over top 30.00

MOTHER-OF-PEARL

☐ Plain, hinged top 65.00

CURRENT
PRICE

PAPIER-MÂCHÉ

☐ Floral design, gilded hinged top 40.00

SILK

☐ Red silk, plain, hand-stitched, slip over top,
    probably Oriental 20.00

SILVER

☐ Gilt with inset pearls, ruby chip in knob of
    hinged lid 115.00

STERLING SILVER

☐ Acorn shape, hinged lid 80.00
☐ Hat box shape, hat top fits down over hat
    brim 85.00
☐ Round with embossed floral design, marked
    "Webster Co." (now Reed & Barton) 80.00
☐ Round with pierced ornate design, marked
    "Webster Co." 90.00
☐ Round, no decoration, English 80.00

SWEET GRASS

☐ Basket, in plain weave with china hand-
    painted thimble, unmarked 30.00
☐ Basket, in plain weave with sterling silver
    thimble 40.00

VEGETABLE IVORY

☐ Round with carved bands 40.00

WOOD

☐ Acorn shape with hinged leaf shape top 48.00
☐ Egg shape 20.00

CURRENT
PRICE

☐ Ligun/Vitae, hand turned, knob at each end,
  late seventeenth century 38.00
☐ Round, carved in leaf design, slip over top,
  European, circa 1865, 3½″ 60.00

Thimble Holders (Stands)

ఘ఻ఘ఻ఘ఻ఘ఻ఘ఻ఘ఻ఘ఻ఘ఻ఘ఻ఘ఻

Thimble holders were considered decorative objects and were displayed accordingly in a house. Thimbles that were made of gold or silver were jeweled and beautifully decorated. They were prized possessions and the needleworker wanted to display these lovely items for others to see. Thus, elaborate, ornate and even whimsical holders were made.

Thimble holders were placed on tables, sewing stands or other pieces of furniture for display. They were made in figural forms such as cats, birds, shoes and children, to name a few. They can also be found in carved, painted and etched pedestal form. Some holders opened up to contain thread and needles. They could be made from metals, wood, ivory or celluloid. Most thimble holders were made to hold a single thimble, but for practical purposes, they were also made to hold more.

Thimble holders are listed alphabetically by the material of which they were made.

Thimble holder. Wood, cover fits down over base, holds two thimbles and four needles, 2⅝" high, 2¼" diameter at base, $25.00.

CURRENT
PRICE

BRASS

☐ Boy, round base, surrounded by six pegs for
thimbles, 4" 90.00
☐ Slipper, purple velvet lining, very ornately
decorated with flowers and leaves, thimble sits
in heel 150.00
☐ Slipper, red velvet lining, very ornately deco-
rated with inset stones in floral pattern, thim-
ble sits in heel 165.00
☐ Walnut shape 135.00

CURRENT
PRICE

CELLULOID

☐ Doll, German 40.00
☐ Man, base is his feet, body and face printed in
   black, thimble sits on head, case opens to hold
   needles 45.00
☐ Man, round base, straight pedestal, round
   printed head, thimble sits on head, stand
   opens to hold needle and thread 35.00
☐ Plain cylindrical holder, opens to hold
   thread 15.00

CHINA

☐ Woman, yellow skirt, white top, facial features
   hand-painted, round base, she holds the thim-
   ble holder 35.00

EMBROIDERED

☐ Slipper, in floral pattern, thimble sits in heel .. 45.00

GLASS

☐ Shoe, with gold and enamel decoration 50.00

METAL

☐ Bird, cast in gold tone, tail holds thimble,
   modern 25.00

SILVER, PLATE

☐ Cat, oval base, with thread and thimble
   holders 65.00

SILVER, STERLING

☐ Cylindrical, pierced in ornate pattern, thimble
   sits on top 70.00

CURRENT
PRICE

WICKER

☐ Cylindrical, plain woven, thimble sits on top ..   18.00

WOOD

☐ Dark, round base, advertising item, seven
  thimble pegs, pincushion 25.00
☐ Dark, round base with thimble peg, fitted for
  small crystal scent bottle 30.00
☐ Mosque, thimble sits on top 25.00
☐ Tree, revolving, three-tiered, 8½″ 50.00
☐ Umbrella, lacquered, hand-painted 40.00

Thimbles

INTRODUCTION

Thimbles have long been very popular to collect. Part of the reason for this is that they are small, easy to display, easy to find in a tremendous variety, and many can be found at a nominal price. However, a more important factor is that many thimbles are miniature works of art, displaying wonderful craftsmanship and great beauty. They are a part of history. The thimble collector will enjoy the benefits of being led into studying metals and other materials used to make thimbles, historical periods, design, fashion, and, perhaps most important, the history of women—their work and their art.

A thimble is a small sewing implement that is bell-shaped and serves two purposes in sewing and needlework. First, it is used to protect the finger on which it is worn and second, to save motion for faster and easier sewing. Most thimbles were designed to fit over the forefinger of either hand, but some were made with open tops, usually called tailor's thimbles, and worn on the thumb of either hand. Most thimbles were made in two parts with the top being joined to the sides. However, onyx and jade ones were usually carved from one piece. Indentations were then added to the thimbles to keep the needle from slipping. Indentations on early ones were done by hand, and, therefore, irregular. Later, they were symmetrically made by a roller. Indentations were found on both parts. China thimbles were the exception, with indentations only on the top. Other additions to the thimble included bands and a rim.

Thimbles have been made since the history of sewing and needlework began. Very early thimbles were undoubtedly made of materials at hand. When tracing their history, it is obvious that a wide range of materials has been used. A partial list includes aluminum, bone, brass, celluloid, China, enamel, glass, gold, horn, iron, ivory, jade, lead, leather, nickel, onyx, pewter, pinchbeck, plastic, porcelain, rubber, silk, silver, steel, tortoise shell and wood. Materials were often combined either for decoration or to provide more strength and durability. Therefore, even though thimbles were made for utilitarian purposes, it is not uncommon to find them with some form of decoration. These can range from the very simple to the ornate. Commonly, jewels, either precious, semiprecious or simulated, were set into the thimble body or top (called a stone top thimble) as decoration.

Of particular interest to many thimble collectors are the gold and silver thimbles of American origin. There have been few goldsmiths and silversmiths known to have made thimbles. Unfortunately, American silver thimbles made during the 1700s were often unmarked. Known American goldsmiths and silversmiths who made thimbles are:

Benjamin Halsted, New York, circa 1766;
Charles Shipman, New York, circa 1767;
Paul Revere, Boston;
James Peters, Philadelphia, Pennsylvania, circa 1824;

George, David and Nathan Platt, Huntington, Long Island, circa 1820s;

Gorham, Webster and Price, Rhode Island, circa 1830;

Ezra Prime, circa 1837–1890;

Edward Ketcham and Hugh McDougall, circa 1875–1932;

Simon Bothers, Philadelphia, Pennsylvania, 1839–present.

Thimble collections can be organized in many ways. A collector may want to concentrate on only thimbles made of particular materials, those with scenes, floral designs, geometric designs, classic designs, scroll or feather designs. Other thimbles that have sparked great interest are advertising thimbles, political campaign thimbles, tailor's thimbles and jeweled thimbles.

Thimbles, like most antiques and collectibles, command the highest price only if they are in mint or excellent condition. This means they should show either no or very little wear. Thimbles that appear worn have much less value. With the relative value in mind, a collector may wish to purchase a worn or reproduced thimble to round out or fill in a collection until a better example or an original is found. Reproductions of some thimbles have been made and undoubtedly more will be made. Old molds are also on the market; at a recent antique show a dealer was selling an old brass mold for $45.

ADVERTISING

The use of thimbles as an advertising medium is a twentieth century phenomenon. With the increasing use of inexpensive materials, such as plastic and aluminum, many businesses could easily afford to have thimbles made for them as giveaway items. The types of businesses using the thimble for advertising are very diverse and the total number made must be staggering. Thimbles made of aluminum date back

Advertising thimbles. *Left to right.* "Prudential Life Insurance," brass, $5.00; "Kauffman Selz Shoes," aluminum, $1.00; "Use Fanchon Flour," aluminum, $2.00; "Diack" (medical supplies) plastic, $1.00.

to the early 1900s. Plastic thimbles were also popularly made and date to the 1930s. Advertising thimbles were also made of silver and brass, but in very limited quantities.

Advertising thimbles are not difficult to find; in fact, you could probably find one in your own home. Because of this, they are a very inexpensive collectible. Plastic and aluminum thimbles will generally fall within the $1 to $4 range. Aluminum thimbles with a colored band, and plastic thimbles with colored tops, will be at the higher end of the range. They can be found at flea markets either alone or in groups. Brass advertising thimbles will generally be found in the $5 to $10 range, while sterling silver thimbles can range from $20 to $25.

Advertising thimbles are listed by the material of which they are made and alphabetically by the company.

CURRENT
PRICE

ALUMINUM

☐ Blazer Oil Co., no colored band, inked
inscription 1.00–
1.50
☐ Bonanza Coffee, "It's Great," colored band,
raised lettering 2.00–
4.00

		CURRENT PRICE
☐	Buick, "Drive a Buick," colored band, inscribed lettering	1.50–2.50
☐	Cadillac Electric Vacuum Cleaners, no colored band, raised lettering	2.00–3.00
☐	Dearborn Laundry, colored band, raised lettering	2.00–4.00
☐	Delco Light "Lightens the Burden of the Housewife," colored band, raised lettering	2.00–4.00
☐	Eagle Laundry, no colored band, raised lettering	2.00–3.00
☐	Emerick Company, undertakers, colored band, raised lettering	2.00–4.00
☐	Excelsior Laundry, colored band, raised lettering	2.00–4.00
☐	Faust Beauty Preparations, colored band, raised lettering	2.00–4.00
☐	Hirschman's Dairy, no colored band, raised lettering	2.00–3.00
☐	"Holland Furnaces Make Warm Friends," colored band, raised lettering	2.00–4.00
☐	Hoover Home Happiness, colored band, raised lettering	2.00–4.00
☐	I. H. Flour, colored band, raised lettering	2.00–4.00
☐	International Harvester, colored band, raised lettering	2.00–4.00
☐	John Hancock Insurance Company, Boston, no colored band, inscribed lettering	2.00–3.00
☐	LaCasa Americana, no colored band, inscribed lettering	1.50–2.50
☐	Maxwell House Coffee, colored band, raised lettering	2.00–4.00
☐	Mid City Trust and Savings Bank, colored band raised lettering	2.00–4.00
☐	Modern Kitchens, Incorporated, no colored band, inked lettering	1.00–1.50

	CURRENT PRICE
☐ Monticello Butane Gas Company, no colored band, inked lettering	1.00–1.50
☐ Mrs. Karl's Fine Bread, no colored band, inked lettering	1.00–1.50
☐ Myer's Furniture Co., no colored band, inked lettering	1.00–1.50
☐ Noll Piano, colored band, raised lettering	2.00–4.00
☐ North American Union Life Assurance Society, colored band, raised lettering	2.00–4.00
☐ NuWay Laundry & Cleaners, colored band, raised lettering	2.00–4.00
☐ Office Supply Company, books, colored band, raised lettering	2.00–4.00
☐ Old Reliable Coffee, colored band, raised lettering	2.00–4.00
☐ Palmetier & Abell, "Thank You," colored band, raised lettering	2.00–4.00
☐ Pieper's Gargoyle Coffee, colored band, raised lettering	2.00–4.00
☐ Pure Oil, "Be Sure With Pure," colored band, raised lettering	2.00–4.00
☐ Purity Nut Margarine, colored band, raised lettering	2.00–4.00
☐ Real Silk Hosiery, Indianapolis, Indiana, no colored band, raised lettering	2.00–3.00
☐ Real Silk Hosiery, Indianapolis, Indiana, colored band, raised lettering	2.00–4.00
☐ Red Diamond Coffee, no colored band, inked lettering	1.00–1.50
☐ Round Oak Furnaces, colored band, raised lettering	2.00–4.00
☐ Sands Gas Water Heaters, no colored band, raised lettering	2.00–3.00
☐ Sheridan Sewing Machines, colored band, raised lettering	2.00–4.00

	CURRENT PRICE
☐ Singer Sewing Machines, colored band, raised lettering	2.00– 4.00
☐ Soft Water Laundry, colored band, raised lettering	2.00– 4.00
☐ Star Brand Shoes, colored band, raised lettering	2.00– 4.00
☐ Star Cleaners, Humboldt, no colored band, raised lettering	2.00– 3.00
☐ Unity Dye Works, colored band, raised lettering	2.00– 4.00
☐ Watkins, "For Goodness Sake Wait for Watkins, Use Watkins Products," no colored band, raised lettering	2.00– 3.00
☐ Yellow Cab, colored band, raised lettering	2.00– 4.00

CHINA

☐ Beer Company, set of three	15.00
☐ General Store, set of four	22.00
☐ Tobacco Company, set of three	18.00
☐ Whiskey Company, set of three	17.00

METAL

☐ Harniss Company	4.00
☐ Tastykake Company	4.50

PLASTIC

☐ American Cleaners, yellow with black lettering	1.00– 2.00
☐ American Home Insurance Company, Topeka, Kansas, blue with black lettering	1.00– 2.00
☐ "Badger Breeders Cooperative Breeding Better Cattle," white with red lettering	1.00– 2.00

	CURRENT PRICE
☐ "Beam World's Finest Bourbon since 1795," pink with black lettering	1.00–2.00
☐ "Beam World's Finest Bourbon," yellow with black lettering	1.00–2.00
☐ "Butter-Nut, the Coffee Delicious," white with black lettering	1.00–2.00
☐ Caloric Stoves, white with black lettering	1.00–2.00
☐ "Celanese Tab is Your Assurance of Quality," orange-yellow with black lettering	1.00–2.00
☐ Crown's, tan with dark brown lettering	1.00–2.00
☐ Eureka, 50th Anniversary, russet with silver lettering	1.00–2.00
☐ Filter Queen, "America's Bagless Cleaner," tan with black lettering	1.00–2.00
☐ Helen Gates Bread, eggshell with black print	1.00–2.00
☐ "Hoover-Home-Happiness," white with black lettering	1.00–2.00
☐ Indiana Roofing, white with black lettering	1.00–2.00
☐ Local Jeweler, white with black lettering	1.00–2.00
☐ Local Laundry, white with black lettering	1.00–2.00
☐ Local Realtor, white with black lettering	1.00–2.00
☐ Luzianne Coffee, white with black lettering	1.00–2.00
☐ Mary Ann Silks and Woolens, white with black lettering	1.00–2.00
☐ Missouri Insurance Company, St. Louis, Missouri, pink with black print	1.00–2.00
☐ Monarch Ranges, white with red top and blue lettering	1.00–2.00

	CURRENT PRICE
☐ One Stop Sewing Shop, white with black lettering	1.00–2.00
☐ Panama-Beaver Inked Ribbons, white with red and blue lettering	1.00–2.00
☐ Panama-Beaver Unimasters, transparent cerise with black lettering	1.00–2.00
☐ Perma-Stone Corporation, white with black lettering	1.00–2.00
☐ Plastic Center, pale pink with black lettering	1.00–2.00
☐ Polly Parrot Max Branovan Quality Shoes for Children, tan with black print	1.00–2.00
☐ Prudential Insurance Company, white with black lettering	1.00–2.00
☐ Rainbow Laundry Inc., tan with black lettering	1.00–2.00
☐ Rod E Popt PopCorn, white with red lettering	1.00–2.00
☐ Schumann & Company, dry cleaners, beige with red lettering	1.00–2.00
☐ Sinclair Oil, with dinosaur, tan with black lettering	1.00–2.00
☐ Sinclair Oil, with dinosaur, white with blue lettering	1.00–2.00
☐ Stage Employees & Movie Operators, white with red lettering	1.00–2.00
☐ Thos. Jackson & Sons, builder's supplies, blue with black lettering	1.00–2.00
☐ Walker's Feeds, white with black lettering	1.00–2.00

SILVER, STERLING

☐ Charlmers Pearls, 1900–1940	25.00
☐ Needlecraft, 1900–1940	28.00

Brass thimble. Plain band, tailor's, marked "14," $8.00.

BRASS

Brass thimbles were generally made for practical purposes. Their indentations run far down their sides. They have also been made in a variety of styles. The most noticeable difference between brass thimbles and all other types is that they were often made with narrow plain strips between their rows of indentations. These are known as two-tier or three-tier thimbles. It is also common for them to have a plain band at the bottom; it can be wide or narrow. Narrow borders were added to the top, bottom or both sides of the band. These borders could be plain, fluted, grooved or beaded. Some rims were even rolled or decorated. These brass thimbles are seldom marked by their makers.

Brass thimbles are listed by three-tier, two-tier and no tier, and then alphabetically by decoration on the band or rim.

THREE-TIER

☐	Narrow plain band, wider demarcation at top, plain rim	5.00– 10.00
☐	Wide plain band, plain rim	5.00– 10.00
☐	Wide plain band, with one row of fluting, plain rim	5.00– 10.00
☐	Wide plain band, some white indentations, plain rim	5.00– 10.00
☐	Wide plain band, plain rim, Germany	5.00– 10.00

TWO-TIER

☐	Narrow tiers, with narrow plain band, plain rim	5.00– 10.00
☐	Wide tiers, with narrow plain band, plain rim	5.00– 10.00
☐	Wide tiers, with wide plain band, hexagonal indentations, plain rim	5.00– 10.00

NO TIERS

☐	Applied butterfly with inset rhinestones, fret band, amethyst top	48.00
☐	Applied castle and drawbridge, scenic	5.00– 10.00
☐	Basketweave design on band, plain rim	5.00– 10.00
☐	Classic design on band with fluting top and bottom, gadroon rim, Austria	5.00– 10.00
☐	Floral design on band, gadroon rim, Austria	5.00– 10.00
☐	Fluted borders	5.00– 10.00

	CURRENT PRICE
☐ Narrow plain band, plain rim, child's	5.00–10.00
☐ Narrow plain band, plain rim, Austria	5.00–10.00
☐ Narrow plain band, plain rim, Germany	5.00–10.00
☐ Narrow plain band with narrow feather border, plain rim, tailor's thimble	5.00–10.00
☐ Narrow plain band with heavy rim	5.00–10.00
☐ Narrow plain band with narrow fluting top and bottom, plain rim	5.00–10.00
☐ Narrow plain band with applied rim, heavy brass	5.00–10.00
☐ Narrow plain band with Greek fan border, plain rim	5.00–10.00
☐ Painted design on band, gadroon rim, Germany	5.00–10.00
☐ Plain with graduated sizes in rows of indentations, plain rim	5.00–10.00
☐ Plain band with braided or faceted rim	5.00–10.00
☐ Plain band with classic border, plain rim	5.00–10.00
☐ Plain band with fluting on top border	5.00–10.00
☐ Plain band with two rows of fluting, plain rim	5.00–10.00
☐ Plain band with three rows of fluting, plain rim	5.00–10.00
☐ Plain band with gadroon rim	5.00–10.00
☐ Plain band inscribed, "The Prudential Life Insurance," plain rim	5.00–10.00
☐ Plain band with zigzag rim	5.00–10.00

	CURRENT PRICE
☐ Scroll design on band, plain rim	5.00–10.00
☐ Scroll design on band, gadroon rim, Germany	5.00–10.00
☐ Scroll design with narrow band below	5.00–10.00
☐ Wide plain band, plain rim, Austria	5.00–10.00
☐ Wide plain band, plain rim, hole at rim to attach to bracelet	5.00–10.00
☐ Wide plain band, beaded edge, plain rim	5.00–10.00
☐ Wide plain band engraved "Good Luck," plain rim	5.00–10.00
☐ Wide plain band with narrow fan trim border, plain rim	5.00–10.00
☐ Wide plain band, fluted narrow rim	5.00–10.00
☐ Wide plain band, fluted wide rim	5.00–10.00
☐ Wide plain band with fluting at top and bottom	5.00–10.00
☐ Wide plain band with four rows of fluting	5.00–10.00
☐ Wide plain band with slanted fluting	5.00–10.00
☐ Wide plain band, inscribed "Her Majesty's Thimble," England	15.00
☐ Wide plain band and narrow unpolished band, plain rim	5.00–10.00
☐ Wide plain band, narrow rolled border top and bottom of band, plain rim	5.00–10.00
☐ Wide plain band with zigzag trim on border, plain rim	5.00–10.00
☐ Wide plain band with short tip	5.00–10.00

Modern China thimble, Christmas motif, green and red on white background, $4.50

CHINA, PORCELAIN

In Europe, China thimbles have been, and are still being, made by some of the leading manufacturers. Many early thimbles were hand-painted by skilled artists and they remain lovely pieces of art. Bone china and porcelain thimbles have always been considered a luxury, as they are not very practical in sewing. However, they are a very colorful addition to any thimble collection. Every book on thimbles contains the story of the $3750 Meissen (Herold Workshop) thimble sold by Christie's of London in 1969. It was ½″ high with a scene of a miniature harbor, complete with six ships, goods on the dock and busy people.

China thimbles are listed alphabetically by the maker.

CURRENT
PRICE

GOEBEL

☐ Hummel, apple girl 22.00

HURLEY

☐ Overall calico background with cherubs
   playing 16.00

CURRENT
PRICE

LEFTON

☐ Overall floral decoration, white background 9.00

LIMOGES

☐ Cream background with birds 15.00

MEISSEN

☐ White background, gilt overall pattern, dome
    top, 19th century 565.00
☐ White background, hand-painted, scenic 110.00
☐ White background, blue band, German in-
    scription, marked with crossed swords 485.00

ROYAL WORCESTER

☐ Bluebirds, sitting on spray of blossoms 45.00
☐ Cream background with birds 40.00
☐ Hand-painted robins, artist-signed 65.00

SPODE

☐ Cream background with heavenly cherubs 30.00

UNMARKED

☐ Currier & Ives print, blue and white 8.00
☐ Floral decoration, hand-painted, artist-signed,
    late 15.00
☐ Fruit decoration with peaches, grapes and
    plums, artist-signed 75.00
☐ Gold raised bird on cream background 55.00
☐ Pink and red roses, blue forget-me-nots, and
    yellow blossom 35.00
☐ Pink and red roses, blue forget-me-nots 40.00
☐ Pink and white roses, gold trim 80.00
☐ Yellow roses in overall pattern 45.00
☐ Yellow roses and blue spray with blue ribbon,
    pale pink background 38.00

COMMEMORATIVE

Thimbles made of materials from aluminum to gold have helped to commemorate events such as fairs, expositions, centennials, and coronations of royalty. They have also been made as souvenirs of the various places we visit.

The thimbles of most interest to the collector are those made of silver or gold and with enameled scenes of events or places of note.

These thimbles have been listed by type alphabetically.

CURRENT
PRICE

COMMEMORATIVE

☐ Laying of the Atlantic Cable, sterling silver 85.00
☐ Liberty Bell, 1976 issue, sterling silver, Simons Bros. 80.00
☐ Queen Elizabeth's coronation, sterling silver, coronation crown with "E" and "R" engraved, England 135.00

SOUVENIR

☐ Empire State Building, New York, sterling silver, embossed with building 25.00
☐ Florida, sterling silver, raised lettering within raised scrolls 25.00
☐ Niagara Falls, sterling silver, embossed scene of falls 25.00

WORLD'S FAIRS AND EXPOSITIONS

☐ Chicago World's Fair, 1933, sterling silver 75.00
☐ Columbian Exposition, 1892, sterling silver, buildings pictured 225.00

CURRENT
PRICE

☐ Columbian Exposition, 1892, sterling silver,
words only, "1492 World's Columbian Exposi-
tion 1892" 200.00
☐ Columbian Exposition, 1892, sterling silver,
words only, "World's Columbian Exposition
1492–1892" 200.00
☐ New York World's Fair, 1939, sterling silver ... 75.00
☐ St. Louis World's Fair, 1904, sterling silver 200.00
☐ San Francisco World's Fair, 1939, sterling
silver 75.00

GOLD

Gold has been used throughout the world from very early
times. However, since gold has also been found in limited
quantities, it has always been considered a luxury.

Gold is considered to be the most malleable of all the metals. This means it is very easy to work with and can be rolled
or beaten into extremely thin layers. Gold in its pure form
(24 karat) is too soft to either work with or wear, and is therefore alloyed with some other metal. Gold with ¾ gold content
and ¼ alloy is termed 18 karat. Gold standards with lesser
gold content are 14 karat, 12 karat, and 10 karat.

Goldsmiths are the artisans who work with gold, and they
have been known to apply the highest standards of craftsmanship and artistry. This is why many of the gold thimbles
made are truly works of art. Actually, at one time, gold thimbles were considered a status symbol. Many were made with
elaborate engraving or embossing, and many with inlaid jewels or stones. Gold thimbles were also made in conjunction
with other metals, such as gold bands on sterling silver. Most
of the gold thimbles to be found today are from the end of the
nineteenth century and beginning of the twentieth century.

Gold and silver thimble. Wide gold band with embossed floral design in high relief, marked "10," $85.00.

Gold thimbles are listed alphabetically by the type of decoration.

CURRENT
PRICE

BIRDS

☐ Engraved birds on band, 14 karat gold 95.00

ENAMEL

☐ Scenic colorful enamel band 160.00

FLEUR-DE-LIS

☐ Engraved fleur-de-lis on band, monogrammed   190.00

FLORALS

☐ Blossom and vine border, decorated rim, Simons Bros. 135.00
☐ Engraved floral design on band 80.00
☐ Embossed floral design on band, Ketcham and McDougall, 14 karat gold 250.00

CURRENT
PRICE

☐ Lilies-of-the-valley and bowknot decoration on
band 185.00
☐ Ornate and intricate floral design on band 225.00

GREEK CLASSIC

☐ Greek classic designs on band, mono-
grammed, Simons Bros. 170.00
☐ Greek classic designs on band, very fine
beaded border, Simons Bros. 195.00

HORSESHOE AND CLOVER

☐ Embossed horseshoe and clover design on
band, monogrammed 80.00

JEWELED

☐ Diamond chips in band, Simons Bros., 14
karat gold 250.00
☐ Semi-precious stones set in band, 14 karat
gold 160.00

LEAVES

☐ Engraved leaf border, 14 karat gold 85.00
☐ Foliage on contrast, Simon Bros. 195.00
☐ Leaf and berry border, faceted rim 80.00
☐ Maple leaf design on rim, Simons Bros. 125.00

PANELS

☐ Applied gold panelled band with contrasting
panels, open space for monogram, Simons
Bros. 115.00
☐ Diamond and panel design on band, indented
beading border, faceted rim 120.00
☐ Plain and engraved panels, arrowhead
trademark 180.00

	CURRENT PRICE
☐ Plain and engraved panels, sterling silver body, Simons Bros.	85.00
☐ Plain panels with geometric space for monogram	80.00
☐ Plain panels, circa 1940	75.00

PLAIN

☐ Basket weave border, 14 karat gold	145.00
☐ Beaded border, lightly engraved rim	95.00
☐ Classic design on rim, monogrammed	85.00
☐ Elongated triangle for monogram	85.00
☐ Fancy border, 24 karat gold	85.00
☐ Grooved rim, F.S. Hoffman, 14 karat gold	150.00
☐ Rococo border, heavy	150.00
☐ Monogrammed, 24 karat gold	95.00
☐ Monogrammed, 14 karat gold	75.00
☐ Monogrammed and dated 1891	135.00
☐ Narrow border, monogrammed, 10 karat gold	75.00
☐ Plain, 14 karat gold	75.00
☐ Plain, 14 karat gold	125.00

PLUMES

☐ Embossed plumes design on band, dated 1827, 10 karat gold	130.00
☐ Engraved plumes design on band, sterling silver body, Simons Bros.	180.00

SCENICS

☐ Buildings engraved within medallions on band, unmarked	170.00
☐ Castle on island engraved on band	135.00
☐ Country scene with house and trees engraved on band, 14 karat gold	225.00
☐ Country scene with house and trees, circa 1940	85.00

CURRENT
PRICE

- ☐ Harbor engraved scene on band, Brogan
  Silversmiths 135.00
- ☐ Seascape engraved scene on border, 14 karat
  gold 110.00
- ☐ House engraved on band, scrolled border,
  14 karat gold 130.00
- ☐ Houses, trees, sunrise engraved on band,
  14 karat gold 190.00
- ☐ Walls of Troy embossed scene on band, Si-
  mons Bros., 14 karat gold 200.00

SCROLLS

- ☐ Embossed scroll design on band, sterling sil-
  ver body, circa 1930, 14 karat gold 65.00
- ☐ Embossed hairline scroll on fluted background
  on band 135.00
- ☐ Embossed intricate scroll design on band,
  sterling silver body 70.00
- ☐ Engraved scroll and floral design on band, in
  Empire style, monogrammed 125.00
- ☐ Wide band with scroll design, English, five
  touch marks 245.00
- ☐ Wide band with scrolls surrounded by trian-
  gles, 14 karat gold 165.00

METALS

Thimbles have been made of various metals, such as lead,
nickel, pewter, pinchbeck and steel. Most of these thimbles
were made for practical use and thus have little or no decoration. They rarely have a marker's mark and therefore it is
very difficult to determine their origin. Furthermore, like
many small items, thimbles were exempt from the 1897 act
requiring the imprint of the country they were made in; it is

often difficult for a collector to trace the origin of a thimble. To complicate the matter, many thimbles found in America have been brought into the country. Keep in mind that many thimbles are here today because they were brought in by immigrants, or after travels from abroad.

Please note that aluminum (advertising), brass, gold, sterling silver, and other silver thimbles are discussed in separate categories.

These thimbles are listed alphabetically by the metal.

CURRENT
PRICE

ALUMINUM

☐ Child's, painted with Goosey nursery rhyme
on wide band 12.00

☐ Child's, small, marked Austria 3.00

☐ Plain, narrow band, unmarked 2.00

☐ Plain, no band, no rim, early 2.00

☐ Plain, wide band, fluted rim, Germany 3.00

IRON

☐ Hand-forged, indentations cover most of thim-   5.00–
ble, no band, tailor's thimble 7.00

☐ Hand-forged, indentations cover ¾ of thimble,   5.00–
no band, small, tailor's thimble 7.00

☐ Hand-forged, indentations cover ¾ of thimble,   5.00–
no band, large, tailor's thimble 7.00

☐ Hand-forged, indentations cover ¾ of thimble,   5.00–
engraved border, tailor's thimble 7.00

☐ Hand-forged, indentations cover ¾ of thimble,   5.00–
large "2" on rim, no band 7.00

☐ Hand-forged, indentations cover ⅔ of thimble,   5.00–
crude joining, tailor's thimble 7.00

CURRENT
PRICE

☐ Lined with aluminum, large indentations   5.00–
cover most of thimble, tailor's thimble 7.00
☐ Lined with aluminum, indentations cover ½ of   5.00–
thimble, tailor's thimble 7.00

METAL, WHITE

☐ Currant vine engraved on band, English 12.50
☐ Fluted rim, indentations cover ½ of thimble,
tailor's thimble 7.00
☐ Marked kewpie 40.00
☐ Thick rim, indentations cover ½ of thimble,
tailor's thimble 8.00

NICKEL

☐ Diamond design on wide band, England 11.00
☐ Fluted border, small indentations cover ½ of
thimble, tailor's thimble 8.50
☐ Indentations cover most of body, tailor's
thimble 6.00
☐ Marked, "SBC" enclosed in Keystone mark 8.00
☐ Narrow band, large indentations cover ¾ of
thimble, tailor's thimble 6.50
☐ Plain band, England 5.50
☐ Plain band, monogrammed 5.00

PEWTER

☐ Child's, inscribed "For a Good Girl" 15.00

STEEL

☐ Fluted rim, large indentations cover ⅔ of
thimble, tailor's thimble 7.50
☐ Indentations cover most of body, no band,
thick rim, heavy, large, tailor's thimble 12.00
☐ Indentations cover most of body, no band,
heavy, large, tailor's thimble 11.00

	CURRENT PRICE
☐ Lined with aluminum, middle section of body covered by indentations, slanted fluting on rim, tailor's thimble	30.00
☐ Middle section of body covered by small indentations, tailor's thimble	10.00

MODERN COLLECTIBLE

Modern thimbles are made out of many materials and in hundreds of styles and forms representing people, nursery tale characters, household items and animals. In fact, many of these are outlandish; it is obvious that they are not functional, but are being made almost entirely to appeal to the thimble collector.

Modern thimbles are being made in America, Europe and the Far East. Thimbles can be of a new variety or antique ones that are reproduced. Reproductions can be made from old molds or dies, new molds copied or from new cast dies. The collector should always be aware that these are reproductions. Some, but not all, are clearly marked. Some thimbles are also being made in "limited" or "collector's" editions. Remember, these types of thimbles, as with most others, should be bought because they are appealing in some way to you, and not for investment purposes.

CURRENT
PRICE

BISQUE

☐ Blue bird figural sits on top nest, pink flowers, green stems and leaves in relief, white background, hole in side to simulate nest, 1½″	9.95
☐ Cat head with shamrock, hand-painted, white background, signed and dated 1986, Roba	8.95
☐ Clown figural bust with ruff, hand-painted red pom-poms and face, white background, 1¾″ ..	6.50
☐ Dog head with shamrock, hand-painted, white background, signed and dated 1986, Roba	8.95
☐ Lamb figural sits on top with small pink flowers, green stems and leaves in relief, white lamb and background, hand-painted, 1⅝″	9.95

☐ Liberty bell figural, blue background, pewter bell and arch decoration in relief, ¾ ″ 7.95

☐ Nutcracker heads, German folklore characters, hand-painted with man-made fur accents, includes Duke, Count, and Earl, 1½ ″, each 14.95

☐ Valentine, hand-painted with hearts and inscribed "Love," dated 1986 and signed, Roba, ⅞ ″ 14.95

BRONZE

☐ Buddha figural, etched detail, 1 ″ 7.95

☐ King Tut figural mask, etched detail, 1 ″ 7.95

CHINA

☐ Alphabet, child engaged in an activity incorporated in letter, 1 ″ 4.95

☐ Bing & Grondahl, annual thimble, cobalt blue background with 24 karat gold hand-painted rim and date, 1 ″ 25.00

☐ Birds, flying in clouds, hand-painted, 18 karat gold trimmed, 1 ″, Fukagawa, Japan 9.50

☐ Book of Kells, gold and green on white background, gold-rimmed, Royal Tara Irish Bone China, 1 ″ 7.00

☐ Crane, 18 karat gold trimmed, 1 ″, Fukagawa, Japan 9.50

☐ Crest with floral medallion, royal blue background, gold trim, nail punch top, gold rim, 1 ″ 8.00

☐ Delft, blue and white, hand-painted, centennial, Statue of Liberty, limited edition, 1 ″ 9.95

☐ Delft, blue and white, hand-painted, Church of Thorn, silver plate with enamel insert, limited edition and dated, ⅞ ″ 7.95

☐ Easter bunny sitting atop grass and colored eggs, hand-painted, 1 ″ 11.95

CURRENT
PRICE

☐ Emerald background with 24 karat gold filigree panels in relief, Germany, 1⅛″ 17.95

☐ Flamingos wading in water, white background
with green reeds, 1″ 8.00

☐ Florals, all-over design, blue flowers on green
stem and leaves, India, 1″ 8.00

☐ Florals, all-over design, lavender and blue, nail
punch top, 1″ 7.00

☐ Floral circle, pale pastel, white background,
gold bands, England, 1″ 5.95

☐ Floral, orange with blue leaves, all edged with
gold, hand-painted, nail punch top, 1″ 7.50

☐ "For Mother" and American beauty rose de-
sign, white background, 1″ 6.50

☐ Gull figural sitting on top thimble, painted
with lighthouse scene, hand-painted, 1⅜″ 11.95

☐ Happy Birthday, blue and lavender balloons
edged with gold on white background, Happy
Birthday banner, 1″ 10.00

☐ Happy Birthday, gift wrapped package in pink
and gold, England, 1″ 5.95

☐ Hearts in red on white background, scalloped
edge, 1″ 8.00

☐ Last Supper, gold top and rim, 1″ 10.95

☐ Man and woman, classical design in 24 karat
gold on cobalt blue background, scalloped rim
and nail punch top, ¾″ 9.50

☐ Mouse figural, sitting on Swiss cheese, hand-
painted, 1½″ 12.50

☐ Mt. Fuji, hand-painted, 18 karat gold trimmed,
1″ 9.50

☐ Mt. Rushmore set of busts of George Washington, Thomas Jefferson, Teddy Roosevelt,
Abraham Lincoln in white, English, 1¼″,
each 8.95

☐ Orchid with reed background, 18 karat gold
trimmed, 1″, Fukagawa, Japan 9.50

CURRENT
PRICE

☐ Oriental floral wreath, 18 karat gold trimmed, 1″, Fukagawa, Japan 9.50
☐ Oriental floral spray with mother-of-pearl finish, gold-banded, 1″ 6.50
☐ Owl in flight, shape sits on top of thimble painted with tree scene, 2″ 9.95
☐ Peter Rabbit, set of 6, Mrs. Tiggy Winkle, Peter Rabbit, Jemima Puddle Duck, Flopsy Bunnies, Benjamin Bunny and the Tailor of Gloster, Wedgwood, set 45.00
☐ Plum blossoms, 18 karat gold rim, Fukagawa, Japan, 1″ 9.50
☐ Shamrock, surrounded with motto "The Lucky Irish Shamrock," gold bands, 1″ 3.50
☐ Shamrocks, five on gold stem, 22 karat gold rims, Royal Tara Irish Bone China, 1″ 7.00
☐ Sombrero figural, slip trail decoration, 1⅞″ diameter 24.95
☐ Stein figural, hand-painted castle scene, pewter lid and thumb rest, 1½″ 22.95

CERAMIC

☐ Cider jug figural, painted schoolhouse scene, replica of stoneware jug, U.S.A., 1¼″ 12.95
☐ Pig, hand-painted in pink with black detailing and blue "#1" ribbon, 1⅛″ 12.95

CLOISONNE

☐ Lotus garden, Oriental birds with floral background, China, 1″ 15.00

COPPER

☐ Presidential, inscribed "Long Live the President G.W.," replica of silver thimble credited to Paul Revere, made for George Washington, antique finish, England, ⅞″ 12.50

☐ Silver-plated with filigree of sterling silver,
deep band, Philippines, 1″ 9.00

GLASS

☐ Cranberry, etched frosted geometric design,
etched band, beaded edge, West Germany, 1″   11.95
☐ Crystal, love bird, etched, nail punch top,
beaded edge, West Germany, 1⅛″ 12.95
☐ Crystal, red, hand-engraved, frosted bird and
branch with flowers and leaves, replica from
the Mary Gallatin Hoppin Collection, Ger-
many, 1″ 15.00
☐ Crystal stein, with gold ornate electroplated
lid and thumb piece, West Germany, 1⅝″ 12.95
☐ Lattice frosted etched over ruby, scalloped
band, beaded edge, West Germany, 1″ 9.95
☐ Mallard, frosted hand etched on ruby, beaded
edge, West Germany, 1⅛″ 14.95
☐ Man and woman holding hands, sprays of
flowers as highlights, frosted hand-etched on
red luster, West Germany, 1⅛″ 14.95
☐ Ruby Hochschnitt (high cut), ruby back-
ground with 24 karat gold filigree panels,
West Germany, 1⅛″ 17.95
☐ Swan, swimming, frosted hand-etched on
ruby, beaded edge, raised nail punch top,
West Germany, 1″ 14.95

METAL

☐ Carousel, gold-plated, canopy top revolves,
nail punch design on body, U.S.A., 1″ 13.95
☐ Edelweiss, painted on body, gold finish metal
top and bands, Austria, ¾″ 10.00
☐ Statue of Liberty head, antique bronze patina
finish, finely detailed, 2″ high × 2½″ wide 12.95

CURRENT
PRICE

☐ Statue of Liberty bust, antique French bronze patina finish, finely detailed, limited and numbered, 1⅝″ high × 1″ wide 8.95

PEWTER

☐ ABC blocks with clown pop up, hand-painted accents, 1¼″ 16.95
☐ Abracadabra figural of bunny in top hat, painted accents, movable eyes, U.S.A., 1¼″ ... 15.95
☐ Bell tower figural, free hanging bell on top opens to nail punch top, England, 1½″ 11.95
☐ Bird cage figural, free swinging yellow bird, painted accents, 1½″ 15.95
☐ Coffeepot figural, hammered design, lid opens to nail punch top, 1″ 11.95
☐ Fireman's hat figural, "FD1 Chief" inscribed, detailed lines, U.S.A., ⅞″ 9.95
☐ Flowerpot with flowers figural, hand-painted accents, two flowers out of flowerpot thimble, 1¾″ 15.95
☐ Granny Goose figural, hand-painted accents, movable eyes, wearing poke bonnet, 1½″ 16.50
☐ Lady Luck, bas relief design, gold finish, lid opens to hold two ⅛″ dice, England, ⅞″ 12.95
☐ Rapunzel in the tower figural, golden braid comes down out of the tower, U.S.A., 1¾″ 12.95
☐ Rocking horse figural, hand-painted highlights, U.S.A., 1¼″ high × 1¾″ long 16.95
☐ "Smallest thimble in the world" in relief lettering, top opens to hold miniature thimble, England, 1″, miniature, 3¹⁄₆″ 10.95
☐ Stanhope with British Royal Prince Henry, inside solid outer case, England, 1″ 14.95
☐ Stanhope with Statue of Liberty pictured, inside solid outer case, England, 1″ 14.95
☐ Teapot figural, copper finish, 1″ 14.95

☐ Teapot figural, hammered design, lid opens to nail punch top, 1″ 11.95

☐ Three little pigs, hinged roof lifts back to reveal pigs, figural wolf sits on outside, hand-painted, England, 1⅛″ 19.95

☐ Windmill figural, hand-painted accents in blue, windmill blades revolve, U.S.A., 1½″ 12.95

☐ Wishing well, figural, water bucket hangs from chain, U.S.A., 1½″ 12.95

☐ Valentine, hand-painted with hearts and inscribed "Love," dated 1986 and signed, Roba, ⅞″ 14.95

POLYMER IVORY

☐ Cat figural, laying down on cushion with long tail wrapped over face, England, 1½″ 11.95

SILVER, PLATE

☐ Norman Rockwell with enamel insert, inscribed "Merry Christmas" and dated 1986, ⅞″ 7.95

SILVER, STERLING

☐ Heart, gold-plated, pierced band, reproduced from the original in Mary Gallatin Hoppin Collection, ⅞″ 32.00

☐ Rabbit, frolicking rabbits in relief, finely detailed, from classic design, ¾″ 36.00

☐ Statue of Liberty, full figure in bas relief, olive branch bands, England, 1″ 26.95

WOOD

☐ Butterchurn figural, hand-painted country scene on natural finish, plunger on top, 2″ 8.95

☐ Cat sitting in window, hand-painted on walnut with maple inlay, 1″ 11.95

	CURRENT PRICE
☐ Cookie jar figural, hand-crafted cherry, hand-painted, 1⅜″	9.95
☐ Church in woods, hand-painted, U.S.A., 1⅛″ ..	12.50
☐ Doctor, soft sculpture head on top, hand-crafted, hand-painted, 1¾″	14.00
☐ Gull figural sitting on piling thimble, hand-painted, cotton rope wound around piling, U.S.A., 1½″	6.00
☐ Jug for moonshine figural, cherry, hand-painted floral decoration, stopper at top, gold finish eye hook forms handle, 1¼″	9.95
☐ Jug for spirits figural, hand-painted moonshiner, removable stopper, U.S.A., 1½″ high × ¾″ diameter	7.95
☐ Milk can figural, hand-crafted cherry, hand-painted with floral decoration, 1″	9.95
☐ Nurse, soft sculpture head on top, hand-crafted, hand-painted, 1¾″	14.00
☐ Ribbon, hand-turned, hand-dipped, enamel coated, various patterns, West Germany, 1″ ...	2.95
☐ Statue of Liberty silhouette against full inlaid maple New York skyline, hand-painted, U.S.A., ⅞″	11.95
☐ Teakettle figural, cherry with wire bail handle, hand-painted floral decoration, U.S.A., 1⅛″ high × 1″ diameter	11.95

POLITICAL

Along with the Harding campaign of 1920 came the political campaign advertising thimble. It is not surprising that this date coincides with the passage of the Women's Suffrage Amendment on August 20, 1920. Because candidates avidly sought the votes of women, the thimble became a convenient medium in which to put across their message. Most political campaign thimbles are made of plastic or aluminum, and the message they carry is printed in ink.

The value of a political thimble is determined by the individual running for office and what that office is. Thimbles for local candidates and state candidates would be less valuable than thimbles with campaign slogans for candidates running for the presidency. Another factor that determines the price of a political thimble is its availability. If very few were made, of course, the price will be much higher.

Political thimbles are listed alphabetically by the candidate.

CURRENT
PRICE

COOLIDGE

☐ "Coolidge & Dawes," aluminum 8.00

EISENHOWER

☐ "Let's Sew It Up for IKE and DICK," 1952 or
1956 .... 12.50
☐ "Let's Sew It Up with IKE-NIXON-POFF,"
1952 .... 9.00

HOOVER

☐ "Happiness with Hoover," plastic 16.00

LAFOLLETTE

☐ "Lafollette and Honest Government" 25.00

NIXON

☐ "Nixon for Congress. Put the Needle in the
P.A.C.," 1946 .... 48.00
☐ "Nixon for Governor," 1962 .... 18.00
☐ "Safeguard the American Home, Nixon for
U.S. Senator," white plastic, 1950 .... 20.00

CURRENT
PRICE

☐ "Sew It Up for Nixon-Lodge, Experience
Counts," 1960 .... 15.00
☐ "Nixon-Lodge Sew It Up," 1960 .... 12.00
☐ "Nixon's the One, Elect Nixon in 1968,"
plastic 14.00
☐ "President Nixon Now More Than Ever,"
1972 .... 9.00
☐ "Nixon-Agnew," 1968 and 1972 .... 4.00
☐ "Nixon-Agnew, '72" 4.00

ROOSEVELT, F.D.

☐ "Roosevelt-Garner," 1936 .... 35.00

ROOT, RUSSELL W.

☐ "Russell W. Root Your Next Mayor," white
plastic 1.00

SMITH, AL

☐ "Al Smith for President," 1928 .... 25.00

WILLKIE, WENDELL

☐ "America for Americans, Willkie for Presi-
dent," Plastic, red, white and blue 28.00

STERLING SILVER

Silversmiths are the artisans who worked with silver. As with
gold thimbles, sterling silver ones were often considered miniature works of art. They were often beautifully engraved,
embossed, enamelled or decorated with jewels. These sterling silver thimbles were often given as a gift to a young girl,
sweetheart, mother or wife. They were often engraved with
initials or a name, and sometimes the date of the gift was

Sterling silver thimbles. *Left to right.* Wide plain band with feathery border, marked "9," $25.00; wide band with paneled medallions, $28.00; wide band with feathery engraving in alternate panels, $32.00.

also inscribed. These lovely sterling silver thimbles were carefully taken care of by the sewer and needleworker and it is certainly possible that many women had "everyday" thimbles at home, and only used their "good" thimbles on sewing circle days.

Sterling silver thimbles are still being made in the same manner. Likewise, they are still considered an appropriate gift. Today, many girls receive them to commemorate a sixteenth birthday, confirmation or graduation.

Silver, in its pure form, is very malleable and would be too soft for most purposes. Therefore, an alloy was added to give it strength and durability. Sterling silver refers to silver that contains 925/1000 parts of pure silver to 075/1000 parts of alloy, which was mainly copper. The term "sterling" was first used in America at about the time of the Civil War.

Sterling silver thimbles are listed alphabetically by the type of decorations.

BIRDS

☐ Birds and vine design engraved on band,
American 25.00
☐ Two birds sitting on a branch, design en-
graved on band 26.00

BUTTERFLIES

☐ Butterflies and leaves, design chased on band,
gold-washed interior 50.00
☐ Fifteen butterflies in flight and poised, design
engraved on band, monogrammed, English 28.00

CHERUBS AND CUPIDS

☐ Cherubs and garlands, design applied on
band, Simons Bros. 88.00
☐ Cherubs and garlands, design engraved on
band, Simons Bros. 30.00
☐ Cherubs and garlands, design engraved on
band, patent November 21, 1905 .... 25.00
☐ Cup and garlands, design applied on band, Si-
mons Bros. 88.00

ENAMEL

☐ Birds with white background on band, Bir-
mingham, England 60.00
☐ Bridge scene with white background, clouds,
lake on band 30.00
☐ Dutch country scene with windmill, house on
band, late 30.00
☐ Farm scene with windmill in panoramic effect
on band, Denmark 35.00
☐ Plain, with wide light blue band and two nar-
row white bands on each side over a guilloche,
Simons Bros. 55.00

	CURRENT PRICE
☐ Roses, red and pink with white background, full enamel body, simulated stone top	60.00
☐ Roses, red and pink, very dainty, with white background, Simons Bros.	40.00
☐ Roses, red and pink with white background, over a guilloche, collapsible	45.00
☐ Vine of green ivy with white background, over a guilloche	40.00

FANS

☐ Fan, design engraved on border, monogrammed	25.00

FLORALS

☐ All-over embossed flower and leaf design	35.00
☐ All-over engraved flower and leaf design, England	30.00
☐ All-over raised flower design, monogrammed on rim	35.00
☐ All-over engraved pansy design	30.00
☐ Aster engraved design on border, monogrammed	25.00
☐ Bleeding heart, raised design on band, circa 1940	25.00
☐ Floral and vine design engraved on band, monogrammed, dated 1894	28.00
☐ Floral and vine, ornate design applied to contrast background	85.00
☐ Floral design engraved on border, wide plain border, beaded rim	25.00
☐ Floral design engraved on narrow band	25.00
☐ Floral design engraved on wide band	26.00
☐ Floral design engraved on wide band, anchor mark	30.00

CURRENT
PRICE

☐ Water lily raised design (large) on wide band,
  gold-washed interior 160.00
☐ Wild rose raised design on wide band, circa
  1930 .... 35.00

GRAPES

☐ Grapes and leaves in raised design on wide
  band 50.00
☐ Grape cluster and leaves design engraved on
  band, monogrammed 25.00

HEARTS

☐ Inverted hearts and panels applied on wide
  band, monogrammed 40.00

JEWELS

☐ Coral stones, set in between fleur-de-lis on
  wide band 85.00
☐ Diamonds and turquoise, set in medallions on
  paneled band, Simons Bros. 250.00
☐ Marquisettes, set in all-over design, old dome
  top, gold lined 135.00
☐ Rubies, three set in chased design 155.00
☐ Semi-precious stones, set in narrow border 60.00

LEAF AND VINE

☐ Leaf design, engraved on wide band, anchor
  mark 30.00
☐ Acanthus leaf design, embossed on band,
  circa 1850 .... 35.00
☐ Currant leaf design engraved on band, mono-
  grammed Ketcham & McDougall 30.00
☐ Leaf and berry design, engraved on band, Simons Bros., monogrammed 45.00

	CURRENT PRICE
☐ Leaf and berry design, engraved on narrow border, monogrammed	25.00
☐ Leaf and circle design, engraved on wide band, anchor mark	34.00
☐ Maple leaf design, engraved on band, monogrammed, dated 1893	30.00
☐ Panel border with leaf motif, monogrammed ..	28.00

PANELS

☐ Narrow panels on wide band	25.00
☐ Plain panels, alternated with ornately engraved panels	34.00
☐ Plain panels on wide band	24.00
☐ Plain panels on wide band, monogrammed	22.00
☐ Plain panels on wide band, H. Muhr Sons	25.00

PLAIN

☐ Advertising, "White Sewing Machine"	25.00
☐ American, circa 1820	115.00
☐ Child's	15.00
☐ Child's, Ketcham & McDougall	18.00
☐ Four plain borders, monogrammed	25.00
☐ Hallmarked, English	30.00
☐ Marked "Sterling-Gunner Mfg.," circa 1890s ..	25.00
☐ Narrow plain band	25.00
☐ Narrow plain band, dated	25.00
☐ Narrow plain band, monogrammed	25.00
☐ Narrow plain band, Simons Bros.	25.00
☐ No design	25.00
☐ No design, monogrammed on rim	22.00
☐ No design, rolled rim	28.00
☐ Rim with bamboo design, monogrammed	25.00
☐ Rim with geometric design, monogrammed, English	25.00
☐ Rim milled and faceted	25.00
☐ Rim, wire	35.00

	CURRENT PRICE
☐ Ring to attach to chatelaine, monogrammed ...	45.00
☐ Sweet grass holder with sterling silver thimble	50.00
☐ Tailor's thimble	34.00
☐ Thread cutter at top, Duke-patented May 15, 1900	35.00
☐ Wide plain band	25.00
☐ Wide plain band, engraved "Mamma"	35.00
☐ Wide plain band, dated 1901	25.00
☐ Wide plain band, monogrammed	24.00
☐ Wide plain band, Simons Bros.	26.00
☐ Wide plain band, Webster Co., monogrammed	25.00

ROCOCO

☐ All-over engraved design, with matching case, circa 1890	135.00

SCENIC

☐ Bridge and boats engraved on band, Gunner Mfg.	30.00
☐ Bridge and towers engraved on band, monogrammed	28.00
☐ Church, pine trees and birds scene engraved on band, Gunner Mfg.	30.00
☐ Country scene, with farm house and silos engraved on band	30.00
☐ Country scene, with farm house, trees, mountains, engraved on band, Simons Bros.	35.00
☐ Country scene, with farm house, trees, mountains, engraved on band, Simons Bros., monogrammed	32.00
☐ Country scene, with house, trees, mountains, lake, engraved on band, Simons Bros., monogrammed	32.00

☐ Country scene, with stone bridge, house and
  mountains, engraved on band, Simons Bros. ..   35.00
☐ Harbor scene engraved on band 30.00
☐ Lighthouse and harbor scene engraved on
  band 30.00
☐ Lighthouse and harbor scene engraved on
  band, monogrammed 30.00
☐ Lighthouse and sailboats engraved on band 30.00
☐ Lighthouse and sailboats engraved on band,
  Gunner Mfg. 32.00
☐ Millhouse, bridge and house scene engraved
  on band, Simons Bros. 35.00
☐ Palm trees and houses engraved on band 30.00
☐ Scenic design engraved on border 30.00
☐ St. Peter's Square, Rome engraved on band,
  monogrammed 30.00
☐ Wild West with buffalo herd, Indian riders,
  campfire, covered wagon and iron horse en-
  graved on band, Simons Bros. 130.00

SCROLL

☐ Scroll design, engraved on wide band, beaded
  rim 28.00
☐ Scroll design, engraved on wide band, open
  top, monogrammed 27.00
☐ Scroll design, raised on wide band, Ketcham &
  McDougall, monogrammed 45.00

STONE TOP

☐ Amethyst top with ornate engraved band,
  German 85.00
☐ Amethyst top with geometric X and rectangu-
  lar design, engraved band 125.00
☐ Carnelian top with engraved floral band, fac-
  eted rim, English 65.00

	CURRENT PRICE
☐ Carnelian top with oval and swag engraved design band	95.00
☐ Jade top with all-over floral design	30.00
☐ Moonstone (simulated) top, monogrammed	35.00

WAFFLE

☐ Waffle engraved design on wide band, England	45.00

OTHER SILVER

Many thimbles were made in silver not using the standard of "sterling." These silver thimbles have a lesser quantity of pure silver and a greater quantity of the alloy. Many were made in Europe and marked "800" or a number in the 800s. This is commonly called Continental silver. The number simply designates the amount of pure silver to alloy. Some silversmiths felt that this type of silver produced a stronger and more durable article. We know that a thimble with any 800 number on it was made in Europe. However, since thimbles were exempt from the 1897 law requiring the imprint of the country of origin, it is very difficult to determine exactly where these thimbles were made. We also know that no thimbles with an 800 number were made in America.

It is interesting to note that although siver thimbles from European and other countries can be as well made and lovely as American ones, they do not command the same interest in the collector's market.

Silver thimbles are listed alphabetically by the type of decoration and, where possible, the origin is noted.

Silver (other) thimbles. *Left to right*. Applied cupid and garlands on wide band, $87.00; embossed leaves and stem de-
sign with applied wirework (Mexican), $14.00.

CURRENT
PRICE

ABALONE

☐ Narrow band of abalone at rim 18.00

DORCAS, DREEMA, DURA

☐ Dorcas, sterling silver on steel core 50.00
☐ Dreema, sterling silver on steel core 125.00
☐ Dura, sterling silver on steel core 125.00
☐ Little Dorcas, sterling silver on steel core 125.00

ENAMEL

☐ Boat scene with shield and arms and band,
  Continental, Germany 70.00
☐ Columbo monument scene on band, (Barce-
  lona, Spain), amethyst top, Continental 95.00
☐ Gondola scene on band, Continental,
  monogrammed 65.00

CURRENT
PRICE

☐ Parthenon scene on band, simulated stone
top 45.00
☐ Roses on white background on band, green
stone top, Continental 65.00
☐ Shield and arms on band, Continental, Puerto
Rico 40.00
☐ St. Peter's Square, scene on band, simulated
red stone top, Continental 75.00
☐ Yellow enamel over a guilloche, carnelian top,
unmarked 65.00

FLEUR-DE-LIS

☐ Applied fleur-de-lis design on band,
unmarked 65.00

FLORAL

☐ Embossed floral design on band, Continental .. 50.00
☐ Embossed floral design on band, unmarked,
possibly Mexico 14.00
☐ Engraved overall floral design, Mexico 14.00

FLUTED

☐ Narrow fluted bands, waffle indentations on
top, tall body, monogrammed, Continental 30.00

JEWEL

☐ Coral set overall, Continental 30.00
☐ Coral set in ornate gilded band, Continental,
circa late nineteenth century 45.00
☐ Green simulated stones set in band, lined in
gold 60.00
☐ Red stones set in wide band, Italian, circa
1900 .... 35.00
☐ Turquoise set in applied band, carnelian stone
top 30.00

CURRENT
PRICE

☐ Turquoise set in applied band, lined in gold 70.00
☐ Turquoise set in band, child's, Continental,
  probably Italy 30.00
☐ Turquoise set in band, Continental 40.00

PIERCED

☐ All-over pierce work, Persian 24.00

PLAIN

☐ Monogrammed, large, possibly India 20.00
☐ Monogrammed, possibly European 20.00
☐ Monogrammed, Mexican, circa 1920 .... 9.50

SCENIC

☐ Castle and tower scene embossed on band 25.00
☐ Sailboats and buildings engraved on band 21.00

STONE TOP

☐ Fluted engraved design on band, amber top,
  Continental 45.00
☐ Initial shield on band, amethyst top,
  Continental 50.00
☐ Medallions in spiral design on band, simulated
  red stone top, Scandinavian 25.00
☐ Plain, synthetic stone cap, Continental 25.00
☐ Plain, synthetic green stone, German 25.00
☐ Plain, synthetic green stone, Sweden 25.00
☐ Plain, synthetic red stone, late 25.00
☐ Plain, synthetic topaz on top, Scandinavian,
  late 25.00
☐ Rose design embossed on band, simulated
  blue stone on top, Scandinavian, late 25.00

Silver (other) thimble. Seven corals alternating with raised fleur-de-lis design, gold washed interior, $42.50.

CURRENT
PRICE

TORTOISE SHELL

☐ Tortoise shell body with wide silver band,
  unmarked 85.00
☐ Tortoise shell inset band 80.00

WIRE WORK

☐ All-over applied wire work, large, Mexico 12.00
☐ All-over applied wire work in scroll design,
  possibly Italian 20.00

Thread

❧❧❧❧❧❧❧❧❧❧

Thread can simply be considered as any fiber of considerable length used to join separate pieces together (as in constructing a garment), to create fabric (as in weaving), to create garments (as in knitting, crocheting) or to decorate fabric. In short, thread is defined as any material that makes it possible to sew. Through the centuries many materials have been used as thread, such as animal sinew, animal intestines, animal or human hair, plant fibers and wire. During the nineteenth century, however, with the Industrial Revolution, advances in technology allowed for the spinning of thread in greater quantities, lengths, and in many varieties. Today, thread is considered to be any fine cord made to a great length from plant, synthetic or animal filaments or fibers. Most thread is made from one or more filaments, of the same or different materials, twisted together. With the advancements in equipment for making thread, many different filaments were combined and twisted in various ways to produce many different types of threads for decorative needlework. In fact, manufacturers even developed different types of threads

Assortment of thread: buttonhole twist, fine crochet cotton, mercerized cotton, darning cotton, pearlized cotton, embroidery silk, mohair yarn, chenille cotton.

and then created a type of needlework which employed the thread. Many threads are used for a very specific type of needlework or sewing; silk embroidery thread (floss), chenille thread, crewel thread (yarn), darning thread (cotton) and buttonhole thread (twist) are good examples.

The most commonly found type of thread is cotton, silk or synthetic thread wound on a spool and used in either hand or machine household sewing. The small household spools made of wood are now a thing of the past and are becoming collectible. They are being collected, with or without the thread, as a small part of history. They are also collected as objects which can be used to make other things. Once empty, the small wood spool has been used to make such things as toys, dolls, Christmas tree chains and the posts for shelves. Creative minds could find many uses for the spool.

Prices on thread and spools of thread are not really established, as they are just becoming collectible. The collector can easily find them at garage sales, household sales and flea markets at a nominal cost.

Thread Holders
and Boxes

❧❧❧❧❧❧❧❧❧❧

Thread holders are containers specifically designed to hold thread, either skein or spool. The purpose of the holder was, and is, to keep the thread in neat, convenient and clean order. Many thread holders have compartments, pegs and drawers to achieve this purpose. Early thread holders were probably hand-made out of fabric with separate pockets for the various threads. Some were made with stitched divisions through which the thread could be slipped. In the eighteenth and nineteenth centuries holders were made of wood, ivory, whalebone, metals or just about any other material that could be formed into a rigid container. The boxes range from very plain to highly ornate. From the mid 1800s and into the twentieth century, small thread boxes were made as advertising giveaways. These little boxes, in particular, are very collectible.

Thread holders are known by several names: thread box, thread holder, spool box, spool holder, spool caddy, and thread caddy. Although they all serve the same purpose, there are slight differences in each:

- •Thread box, a container to hold loose thread or skeins.
- • Spool box, a container to hold spools of thread.
- • Spool holder, a container with a number of pegs or compartments to keep the spools separated.
- • Spool caddy, same as a spool holder, but designed to be easily portable.
- • Thread caddy, same as a thread box, but again designed to be easily portable.

Thread holders are listed alphabetically by the material of which they are made, with the exception of advertising boxes which are listed separately.

	CURRENT PRICE

ADVERTISING

☐ Brook's "Glace Soft Finish Thread," lithograph of Victorian woman on lid, 3½"	45.00
☐ Clark's O.N.T., lithograph of Western scene on lid, 4¾" × 3½"	40.00
☐ Clark's O.N.T., lithograph of lake scene on lid, tummel	50.00
☐ Clark's O.N.T., contains pegs for eight spools, needles and thimble, Clark label	28.00
☐ Clark's O.N.T., wood, 2" × 3¾", Clark label ..	40.00
☐ Clark's O.N.T., "Boilfast," tin, 3" × 3", Clark label	35.00
☐ Coats, J. & P., advertising label under lid, tin, 5¼" × 3½"	25.00
☐ Coats, J. & P., crochet and darning cotton, Coats label, 3" × 3½"	40.00
☐ Coats, J. & P., chromolithograph of kittens on lid, turned maple, 2½" × 4"	75.00
☐ Rice's Sewing Silk, wood, Rice label	25.00

	CURRENT PRICE
☐ Round Robin, contains pegs for six spools	12.00
☐ U.S. Playing Card Co., plastic, company label	15.00

BRASS

☐ Embossed octagonal ring, three section spool holder, needle holder and thimble holder	25.00
☐ Kate Greenaway type figure	75.00
☐ Three-tier stand, contains pegs for five spools, three scrolled feet, 12″	320.00

CELLULOID

☐ Cat with long stretched neck to hold spools	35.00
☐ Girl's head, red thimble hat unscrews to interior thread holder, Germany	40.00

CAST IRON

☐ Rotating shelf, contains pegs for nine spools and fitted pincushion, decorative fitted base	70.00

IVORY

☐ Acorn shape, opens to hold one small spool	75.00
☐ Barrel shape, opens to hold one small spool	85.00
☐ Round, carved, opens to hold one small spool .	34.00
☐ Three graduated tiers, scrimshaw, center of wood star, early nineteenth century, 6¼″ high	1125.00

MAHOGANY

☐ Box with one secret drawer, 7″	60.00

MAPLE

☐ Coffee grinder shape, one spool drawer, pin-
cushion on top of lid 35.00
☐ Round base, fitted center pincushion, circa
1880 ....   35.00
☐ Two-tier, holds spools, turned top finial and
feet, 8¼" 50.00
☐ Two-tier, tiger maple, early 1800s 40.00

PAIRPOINT SILVER

☐ Cat shape, holds thread and thimble, small 55.00

SILVER, PLATE

☐ Three-tier, very plain, 14" high 250.00
☐ Three-tier, women's figural heads on top,
marked Manning & Borman, piece resilvered,
14" high 257.00

SILVER, STERLING

☐ Round, covered, embossed floral decoration,
opens to hold one small spool 135.00
☐ Round, hinged, embossed scroll decoration,
opens to hold one small spool 135.00
☐ Round, covered, small figural cherubs on top,
opens to hold one small spool 165.00

UNIDENTIFIED WOOD

☐ Beehive shape, three turned feet, bee finial 75.00
☐ Capstan shape, six parts each with pewter lid,
red finish 75.00
☐ Coffee grinder shape, spool drawer contains
pegs for eight spools 45.00

☐ Pinwheel carved, 3″ × 3½″ 40.00
☐ Round base holds pegs for six spools, three
turned feet, pincushion in center, 4″ 45.00
☐ Round, plain revolving base 20.00
☐ Round base with spool pegs, fitted thimble
and scissors holders 65.00

WALNUT

☐ Box, contains pegs for five spools, pincushion,
thimble holder and thimble, base has one
drawer, 4½″ × 6½″ 60.00
☐ Pedestal, wire spokes to hold spools, pincush-
ion on top, base has one drawer 60.00
☐ Round, contains brass pins for ten spools, pincushion fitted in center 65.00
☐ Three-tiers, contains pegs for 16 spools, large
pincushion on top, fitted with five thimble
holders, button feet 75.00
☐ Three-graduated tiers, pincushion on top, con-
tains whale bone pegs for 29 spools. Base has
four drawers with turned whale bone knobs,
circa 1870s, 14″ high 575.00

WHALE BONE

☐ Round, plain, opens to hold one spool 85.00
☐ Scrimshaw, opens to hold one spool, 3″ 135.00

Thread Waxers

Beeswax was used as a medium to strengthen early threads. It was also used to smooth the thread so that it could more easily be drawn into and out of the fabric being worked. Containers made of ivory, bone, metal or wood were used to hold the beeswax. Very often a smaller receptacle was added to hold a more convenient amount. Most of these containers were made during the eighteenth and nineteenth centuries. Many were conveniently made as part of a fitted sewing or needlework box. However, by the late nineteenth century, thread wax containers were no longer being made. For this reason they are very rare. Collectors must always be alert, since they are very often not recognized.

CURRENT
PRICE

☐ Cylinder shape with ivory disc base, beeswax
in the middle, carved mother-of-pearl top 55.00
☐ Cylinder shape with Tunbridge ware, with
geometric design base, beeswax in the middle,
and velvet pincushion on top, 2″ high 65.00

☐ Cylinder shape with wood base and wood top,
with inlays on mother-of-pearl and brass in
floral design, circa 1850 .... 75.00

Thread Winders

Thread winders provided a convenient method of keeping threads sorted. They were small objects, usually from one inch to three inches, and generally made from bone, ivory, mother-of-pearl or wood. Winders were cut into various shapes that could conveniently hold the thread as it was hand-wound around it. They often came in such interesting shapes as stars, snowflakes and scalloped rounds. Square, round and rectangular thread winders with indentations were also used. Interesting to note is that many sewing boxes, particularly during the eighteenth and nineteenth centuries, were fitted with several thread winders.

   Thread winders are listed alphabetically by the material of which they were made.

CURRENT
PRICE

BONE

☐ Rectangular, with slightly rounded sides and
   concave ends, 2″ 7.50

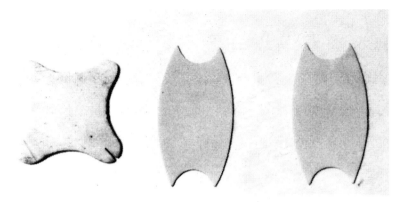

Thread winders, *Left to right.* Ivory, 1⅛″, $25.00; bone, ⁹/₁₆″ long, $7.50; wood, ⁹/₁₆″ long, $4.00.

	CURRENT PRICE
☐ Rectangular, with squared-off ends that contain a notch, slightly concave sides and ends ..	10.00
☐ Square, with concave sides, 1¼″ × 1¼″	7.50

CARDBOARD

☐ Eight-pointed star, advertising, early 1800s	25.00

IVORY

☐ Fish, 1½″ long, circa 1750, English	30.00
☐ Round, with pierced and scalloped border	40.00
☐ Snowflake	45.00

MOTHER-OF-PEARL

☐ Eight spokes with floral engraving, 1¾″, nineteenth century, Chinese	65.00
☐ Round with scalloped border	45.00

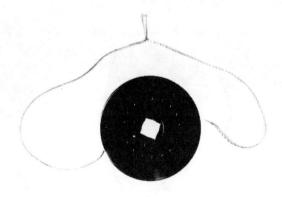

Thread winder. Lace bobbin, weaver's lace loom, brass, $18.00.

	CURRENT PRICE
☐ Round with eight very deep rounded indentations	60.00
☐ Round with small notching around edge	40.00

SANDLEWOOD

☐ Round, hand-carved, four rounded indentations	9.00
☐ Square, hand-carved, rounded indentations on four sides	12.00

WHALE BONE

☐ Lace bobbin, scrimshaw handle, loop of Venetian beads at top, 3½″ long	60.00

Tracing Wheels

❀❀❀❀❀❀❀❀❀❀❀

The tracing wheel is a hand tool dating back to the 1860s. It is still considered a fairly recent innovation. Basically, the tracing wheel was used to do exactly what its name implies, that is, to trace a pattern. It had a revolving disc at the end of a spur, with sharp marginal points (rowel) set into a shaft of metal (steel, brass or iron). There was also a handle for

Tracing wheel. Steel rotating wheel in wood turned handle, 5⅛″ long, $8.00.

easy maneuvering. The fabric to be worked was laid on a flat surface, tracing paper was placed on top of the fabric and the pattern on top of that. The tracing wheel transfers from the tracing paper, to the fabric, colored pin-prick marks. It is clear to see that this was a very nice tool to have around. Patterns could be copied from magazines, papers and paper patterns.

	CURRENT PRICE
☐ Nickel-plated metal handle, steel shaft and wheel, collapsible	4.00
☐ Wood handle, brass shaft, steel wheel, 6¼″	12.00
☐ Wood handle, cast-iron shaft, steel wheel, 6″ ..	8.00
☐ Wood handle, steel shaft and wheel, 7″	5.00

Trade Cards

❀❀❀❀❀❀❀❀❀❀

Advertising trade cards were very popular giveaways for a wide range of businesses and concerns. Most were made in a rectangular shape but some were cut in figural form. Trade cards were generally rather small, about 2 inches × 4 inches, but could be as large as 7 inches × 10 inches. They were particularly popular from the 1880s to the 1890s. Most trade card pictures were made from hand-drawn art and and were very colorful and imaginative. With the advent of lithography it was now both easy and economical to reproduce pictures on paper in color, and trade cards became particularly impressive and popular. Unfortunately, by 1900 this wonderful source of information and beauty was losing its charm, and by 1910 it was virtually a lost art. Luckily, many of these trade cards were made in series and were avidly collected, traded and saved in scrapbooks.

As with any paper collectible, the trade card that is crisp, clean, has no paste residue on the reverse, and no bends or folds will command the highest price. A trade card that shows considerable wear has very little value.

Trade cards. *Top.* "Facsimile of Embroidery Done on the Davis Vertical Feed Sewing Machine," Watertown, NY, $3.50. *Bottom.* "For Hand and Machine" Coats thread, $4.00.

Trade cards are listed alphabetically by the advertising manufacturer.

CURRENT
PRICE

BRAINERD AND ARMSTRONG SILK THREAD

☐ Rectangular card, with lithograph picture of
children playing 8.00

CLARK'S O.N.T. THREAD

☐ Rectangular card, with lithograph picture of
two little boys using spool of thread to fly a
kite, one boy in air and the other holding
thread from ground 6.00
☐ Rectangular card, with lithograph picture of
child in blue dress, white smock, holding
drum with Clark logo on top 4.50
☐ Spool-shaped card, with die-cut picture, adver-
tising on back 4.00
☐ Spool-shaped card, with lithograph picture of
girl in pinafore surrounded by spools of
thread 7.00
☐ Spool-shaped card, with lithograph picture of
mother and child, "Nothing stronger can there
be, than mother love and O.N.T." 8.00
☐ Square-shaped card, with lithograph picture of
Jumbo the elephant 5.00

COATS, J.P.

☐ Rectangular card, with lithograph picture of
boy and girl in black silhouette, boy carrying
colored paper lantern on stick, spool in upper
right 4.00
☐ Rectangular card, with lithograph picture of
four frogs on bicycles 18.00
☐ Rectangular card, with lithograph picture of
frog soldiers marching across lily pads, circa
1890 .... 5.00
☐ Rectangular card, with lithograph picture of
girl powdering nose of frowning dog, store
cabinet in background, box of thread on floor,
best six cord 6.00
☐ Rectangular card, with lithograph picture of
Gulliver being tied up with thread by the Lili-
putians, story on reverse 3.00

CURRENT
PRICE

☐ Rectangular card, with lithograph picture of
Jumbo the elephant 4.00
☐ Spool-shaped card, with lithograph picture of
young girl hanging wash and young boy rest-
ing on spool of thread 3.50

CORTICELLI SILK THREAD CO.

☐ Rectangular card, with lithograph picture of
three young ladies lassoing a young man (with
thread), "The Perils of Leap Year" 8.00
☐ Rectangular card, with lithograph picture of
four kittens playing with thread 6.50

DAVIS SEWING MACHINES

☐ Rectangular card, with lithograph picture of
vertical feed sewing machine 6.00

DOMESTIC SEWING MACHINES

☐ Rectangular card, with lithograph picture of
bride and groom with sewing machine, circa
1882 .... 3.00
☐ Rectangular card, with lithograph picture of
Palmer Cox Brownies in tree 8.00
☐ Rectangular card, with lithograph picture of
two girls in carriage stopping to read sign advertising sewing machine 5.00

EUREKA SILK MANUFACTURING COMPANY

☐ Rectangular card, with lithograph picture of
cottage and country garden 2.25

GOLDEN EAGLE KNITTING WOOLS

☐ Rectangular card, with lithograph picture of
woman in front of mirror, Trafalger Works,
Halifax 3.00

HOME SEWING MACHINES

☐ Rectangular card, with printed picture of car-
toons promoting features of machine, local
dealer's advertising on reverse 4.00

KEEN KUTTER

☐ Fan-shaped card with printed advertising 2.00

KEER & CO. EXTRA SIX CORD SPOOL COTTON

☐ Rectangular card, with lithograph picture of
"The Fox and the Stork," Aesop's Fables,
story on reverse 6.00

LEADER SEWING MACHINES

☐ Rectangular card, with lithograph picture of
girl with parasol waving to boat with
"Leader" printed on sail 3.00

MERRICK

☐ Spool-shaped card, with lithograph picture of
girl in hammock, advertising on reverse 4.00

NEW HOME SEWING MACHINES

☐ Rectangular card, with die-cut scene of
woman holding bouquet of flowers, her daugh-
ter and doll at her feet, sewing machine to the
side, circa 1890 .... 18.00
☐ Rectangular card, hold-to-the-light card, sew-
ing machine with parts cut out to background
that shows through 8.00

☐ Rectangular card, with lithograph picture of Victorian girl on day bed dreaming, "New Home Dream," machine pictured in center top 4.00

SINGER SEWING MACHINES

☐ Rectangular card, with lithograph picture of cats chasing mouse in front of machine, advertising on back 4.50

☐ Rectangular cards, from Columbian Exposition, lithograph, original box, set of 36 .... 60.00

☐ Rectangular cards, country series, lithograph picture of person in native costume standing in front of sewing machine, story on back, 1892 .... 4.50

☐ Rectangular card, with lithograph picture of sewing machine, advertisement on back 7.50

STANDARD ROTARY SHUTTLE SEWING MACHINE

☐ Rectangular card, with lithograph picture of two young girls in half portrait 3.00

STAR EMBROIDERY SILK

☐ Rectangular card, with lithograph picture of star with embroidered flowers 2.25

WHEELER & WILSON SEWING MACHINE

☐ Rectangular card, with lithograph picture of mother and child, mother at machine, child in crib 5.00

WHITE SEWING MACHINE

☐ Rectangular card, with center oval picturing two women and child and sewing machine 5.50

CURRENT
PRICE

☐ Rectangular card, with picture of winter scene in star shape, and rose and blue bird, advertising on reverse 3.00

☐ Rectangular card, with lithograph picture of children playing in background, sewing machine in front, advertising on reverse 5.00

WILLIMANTIC THREAD

☐ Rectangular card, with lithograph picture of Brooklyn Bridge and ships in background, advertising on reverse 6.00

☐ Rectangular card, with lithograph picture of cupid flying around the world and tying it with thread 4.50

☐ Rectangular card, with lithograph picture of Jumbo the elephant and circus parade 12.00

☐ Rectangular card with lithograph picture of little girl in white dress, advertising on reverse .. 3.00

Work Baskets

❖❖❖❖❖❖❖❖❖❖❖

A work basket is simply a convenient container that can be easily carried around while holding the tools and materials being used for a sewing or needlework project. Work baskets of one type or another have probably been used as long as people have been doing sewing and needlework. They may be found with fitted compartments for specific tools, but more often are simply a plain basket. They have been made out of many materials and in many different ways. However, today you will most commonly find work baskets that have been made from raffia, splint wood, wicker or sweet grass. These are the materials that were most often used in the weaving of baskets. Raffia is the fiber from the raffia palm, wicker is the pliable twig from the various willow trees, splint is a thin strip of wood and sweet grass is strong, dried grass.

At the present time, probably the most common type of work basket found on the market, and consequently the least expensive, is the basket made from sweet grass. It can easily be found at auctions, flea markets, garage and house sales, and from dealers. If you are lucky, the basket will be filled with thread, needles, pins, buttons and other sewing and needlework implements. This can provide much enjoyment in the sorting and classification of these accessories.

Work baskets are listed alphabetically by the material of which they are made.

CURRENT
PRICE

CARDBOARD

☐ Eight-sided, fabric-lined, collapsible, Victorian   38.00

CHINTZ

☐ On metal frame, with matching needle case, circa 1840, no cover 50.00

NEEDLEPOINT

☐ On leather frame and with leather handle, 15″ × 9″, no cover 95.00

RAFFIA

☐ Woven, with handle and needlepoint cover 25.00

REED

☐ Woven, with reed handle, no cover 15.00
☐ Woven body, three legs, solid wood cover 40.00

SPLINT

☐ Attached cloth pockets and scissors 165.00
☐ Heart shape with wire hinged top, 6″ × 6″ 20.00
☐ Lined with blue satin, fitted for beeswax and needle case, no cover 75.00
☐ Lined, fitted cover, 5″ × 3½″ 70.00
☐ Nantucket, swing handle, no cover, 13″ 275.00
☐ Picket fence design, lined, circa 1870, 4½″ × 11″ 95.00
☐ Shaker, caned inner rim, fitted with needle holder 55.00

Work basket. Woven raffia in natural color with blue, tan
and pink trim, hinged lid, blue satin lining, circa 1920s,
$25.00.

	CURRENT PRICE
☐ Shaker, four interior baskets, dated 1872	425.00
☐ Shaker, lined, with cover, 5½″ sq.	85.00
☐ Shaker, Sabbathday Lake stamp, silk-lined, needle case	275.00
☐ Shaker, splint handles, no cover	55.00
☐ Shaker, splint handles, inside needle holders, no cover	50.00

STRAW

☐ Pink ribbon and lining, hexagonal, Shaker, needle case, pincushion, emery, beeswax	250.00

SWEET GRASS

☐ Chinese, coin and glass bead design on cover, 5¾″	22.00

Work basket. Wicker woven in natural color, cover fits down over bottom, 9″ × 6¾″ × 2¾″, $14.00.

	CURRENT PRICE
☐ Chinese, coin design on cover, attached tassels	33.00
☐ Chinese, attached coins on cover, 8″	18.00
☐ Chinese, covered	15.00
☐ Chinese, covered, 10″	25.00
☐ Filled with pincushion, needle case, crochet hook	28.00
☐ Shaker, Canterbury, circa 1890, 2″ × 4½″	175.00

WICKER

☐ Bead and coin trim on cover, 9″	30.00
☐ Child's, with handle, 5½″ × 2½″	18.00
☐ Coin design on cover, 9″	22.00
☐ Covered, 12″	22.00
☐ Filled with needles and thread	30.00
☐ Lined, satin-quilted	80.00
☐ Lined, cretonne, scalloped rim, no cover, 8″	15.00
☐ Picnic basket-shaped, D.M.S. Floss	180.00

	CURRENT PRICE
☐ Pouch-shaped, beaded decoration, 9″ × 4½″	40.00
☐ Standing, 29″	85.00
☐ Tapered body, fitted cover	35.00
☐ Victorian, lined, fitted with scissors, pins, three legs	110.00
☐ Victorian, two-tier insert, large	150.00

Workboxes

❀❀❀❀❀❀❀❀❀❀

From very early times, some container was needed to keep all the tools that were required for sewing, mending and needlework in one place. The earliest containers that could easily be carried from place to place were baskets. Generally, they were uncovered and unfitted with perhaps some sort of lining. They not only held tools, but fabric and other objects that were being worked as well (see Work Baskets). Later, the workbox was designed to more conveniently hold sewing and needlework implements. Workboxes were made in round, oval and square shapes. They were made of solid, firm materials such as wood, tin, silver or stiffened leather. They almost always had a cover, lid or door.

During the early eighteenth century, workboxes were made in Europe as very decorative and elaborate objects. Beautiful woods and wood veneers were used in the construction of the box. The box itself was often decorated with inlays of wood veneers, mother-of-pearl, ivory, gold or brass. Sometimes it was studded with cut stones or faceted steel. Many had lift-out trays that were lined with velvet or satin and had formed receptacles for the specific tools, such as scissors, thimbles, bodkins, needle case and more. Fitted areas were also added in some boxes for items that were considered essential to household tasks, but were nonsewing items such as vinaigrettes, pencils and picks. Fitted elaborate workboxes were also made to hold all the necessary tools used to perform a specific sewing or needlework task.

Workboxes can be found that were for lacemaking, tatting and embroidery. Today it is very difficult to find any of these boxes with all their tools intact.

In contrast, early American-made workboxes were generally simple, plain boxes. Quaker and Shaker tradition did not allow for elaborate decoration. The early settlers did not have the time, tools or materials to make fancy boxes. Occasionally, an early workbox can be found that had been painted for decoration. Any elaborate workboxes found here were undoubtedly imported.

Workboxes are listed alphabetically by the material from which they are made, with the exception that Shaker workboxes are listed separately.

CURRENT
PRICE

BRASS

☐ Casket shape, with brass beading 165.00
☐ Engraved, octagon, three section spool holder,
   needle holder, thimble holder, late 25.00
☐ Embossed, thimble holder, thread holder,
   needle holder, Germany 24.00

CHERRY

☐ Lift-out tray, inlaid with sprays of shamrocks,
   $6\frac{1}{2}$″ × $10\frac{1}{2}$″ × 4″ 185.00

CURRENT
PRICE

IVORY

☐ Fitted for thread, thimble, punch holder,
small 65.00
☐ French, inlaid with 14 karat gold decoration,
circa 1840 .... 1825.00

LACQUERED

☐ Chinese, gold-decorated, nineteenth century,
14¼" long 325.00
☐ Chinese, sterling silver handles, ivory-carved
spindles, 1805 .... 3500.00
☐ Oriental, brass claw-shaped feet, ivory grill
work sides, 10" × 17" 950.00

LEATHER

☐ Moroccan, lift-out divided tray, covered center
box, brass feet, brass pulls 525.00
☐ Silver trim, satin-lined, plain interior 35.00
☐ Sterling silver fittings 95.00

MAHOGANY

☐ Baleen whale trim, fittings for knitting case,
11", oval 450.00
☐ Bird's Eye maple veneer drawer, six ivory
eyelets 130.00
☐ Brass inlay, velvet lift-out tray 95.00
☐ Cherry and mother-of-pearl inlay, lift-out
tray 850.00
☐ Domed lid, plain 350.00
☐ Flame grain veneer, beveled edge lid, fitted
lift-out tray, paper lining 65.00

Workbox. Mixed woods, unusual with inked and grooved decoration, 12″ × 15½″ × 9″, circa early 1900s, $45.00.

CURRENT
PRICE

☐ Rosewood, ivory, mother-of-pearl, abalone inlays, two drawers, center well, two lift compartments, eight spool holders, circa 1840, 5¼″ × 12″ × 9″ 5700.00

☐ Rosewood, ivory inlays, two-tier, ivory feet and knobs, eight thread eyelets, removable top with pincushion, thimble holder, circa 1840, 6″ × 7″ 785.00

CURRENT
PRICE

MAHOGANY VENEER

☐ Inlaid wood veneer lid, 4″ × 8″ × 11″ 40.00
☐ On pine, flame grain, beveled edge lid, fitted
    tray, blue and white printed paper lining. 50.00

MAPLE

☐ Box with lift lid, spindle and grill work sides,
    oval 19 × 15″ 65.00
☐ Coffee grinder shape, one drawer, pincushion
    top 35.00
☐ Curly maple, Shaker, two-tier, spool rods over
    one drawer, 8″ 235.00

METAL

☐ Empire, gilt, fitted interior, 10″ diameter 110.00
☐ Red velvet pincushion on top 30.00

MIXED WOODS

☐ Walnut, maple and cherry, two-tiered, one
    drawer, top opens to compartment for spools
    and eight ivory eyelets, pincushion on base,
    5¼″ × 7″ 75.00
☐ Walnut, maple and cherry, lift-out tray fitted
    with eyelets, 5″ × 7″ 65.00
☐ Walnut, maple and cherry, one drawer, top
    spool compartment 65.00

MOIRE, GROSGRAIN

☐ Metal frame, rope handle, circa 1935, 8″ 30.00
☐ Metal and cardboard frame, knitting needles,
    complete with needles, 6″ × 15″ 35.00

OAK

☐ Bookcase shape, mirror front 195.00
☐ Cupboard, mini-stepback, with sliding doors,
  12″ 100.00
☐ Pincushion top, lift-off top holds 20 spools of
  thread, 12″ × 3″ 75.00

PAINTED WOOD

☐ Black, three-drawer, glass drawer pulls, spool
  holders, pull-out shelf on bottom, circa 1910 .. 210.00
☐ Blue to black paint, two trays, circa 1839,
  9″ × 10½″ 95.00
☐ Marbleized enamel, three section spool, needle
  holder and thimble holder 19.00
☐ Polychrome florals and leafy decoration, pale
  yellow base, decorated fitted interior, mirror
  under lid 375.00
☐ Portrait of child, dog, and flowers, hand-
  painted, 12″ 225.00
☐ Primitive scenic painting, top, floral and sprig
  painting on sides, 12″ 245.00

PINE

☐ Shell-covered, lined, 5″ × 6″ 22.00

ROSEWOOD

☐ With inlays, 9½″ × 8″ 38.00

SCRIMSHAW

☐ Whalebone inlays, very intricate, mirror inside
  lid, lift-out fitted tray, circa 1840 .... 475.00

SATINWOOD

☐ Original lacemaking implements, English,
circa 1825 .... 2100.00

SHAKER

☐ Box within box, plain boxes 225.00
☐ Curly maple, two-tiered, spool rods on top tier,
drawer, 8″ 235.00
☐ Domed, plain 285.00
☐ Enfield, walnut, four fitted sliding trays, top
lift 100.00
☐ Handle, fitted for pincushion, needle case,
lined, 7½″ 190.00
☐ Handle, hoop type, silk lining, 5½″ × 2¼″ 85.00
☐ Leather, fitted, 6½″ 125.00
☐ Leather ends, 4″ × 1½″ 85.00
☐ Lipstick-red color, pincushion cover, 1846 in-
scription inside (record set at auction) 4950.00
☐ Octagon, pink silk-lined, Maine 190.00
☐ Plain, three-finger construction, copper tracks 225.00
☐ Satin lining, Sabbathday Lake, Signed 235.00
☐ Wood inlaid with geometric design on lid, inte-
rior blue paper lining, fitted tray 3¾″ × 7⅞″
× 11″ 95.00

UNKNOWN WOODS

☐ Cradle form, small 18.00
☐ Dome top, fitted interior, 4¼″ × 2½″ 25.00
☐ Dovetailed, cane trim, lined, 7″ × 12″ 35.00
☐ Dovetailed, white porcelain knobs 50.00
☐ Lacemaker's set, lined and fitted, bone han-
dles, six piece 135.00
☐ One drawer, calico pincushion top 40.00
☐ One drawer, spool tree, pincushion, porcelain
knob, 6″ × 13″ 95.00

Workbox. Mahogany, dark finish, pegged construction, sliding interior tray, 24½″ high × 11⅜″ wide × 11½″ deep at top, $85.00.

	CURRENT PRICE
☐ Seamstress case, portable, dark finish, two chintz shelves on one side, one pocket each side at bottom, case is hinged and divides in half, brass handles, 15″ × 18″	85.00
☐ Thimble holder on top, workbox is bottom	75.00
☐ Tiered, one drawer, lift top, eight spool spindles, 5½″ × 7″	65.00

☐ Turned, tree form on top to hold thread, pincushion top, nailed drawer base, 13½" 110.00
☐ Turnbridge Ware, stained wood inlays,
10½" 195.00

WALLPAPER OVER WOOD

☐ Plain box 86.00

WALNUT

☐ Bird's eye maple veneer, dovetailed drawers ... 185.00
☐ Book shape, secret opening 65.00
☐ Brass inlay, purple velvet lining on lift-out
tray 85.00
☐ Burl inlay of ship and lighthouse on lid,
English, late eighteenth century, 3¼" 145.00
☐ Fabric, padded lid, 7" × 15" 55.00
☐ Gilt, figural ring 14.00
☐ Mixed wood inlay, in diamond and triangle
pattern, lift-out velvet lined tray, mirror under
lid, 9" × 15½" 210.00
☐ One drawer, spool holders, pincushion on top,
4½" × 6½" 45.00
☐ One drawer, spool holder, and pincushion on
top, 4½" sq. 44.00
☐ One drawer, spool holder, pincushion on top,
original label, 4½" × 7½" 48.00
☐ Satin-lined, key lock, plain box, 7¾" × 10¾" 85.00
☐ Six section, lift-out tray, lock, 7¾" × 11¼" 95.00
☐ Spool holder, pincushion, thimble holder and
fitted thimble holder 55.00

Yarn Winders
(Skein Holders)

❀❀❀❀❀❀❀❀❀❀❀

The spinning wheel spun continuous lengths of yarn. The yarn winder, or skein holder, was the tool that took the spun yarn and wound it into usable skeins (hanks) or lengths and/ or measured the yarn. Of course, to wind yarn, two hands could be held apart at the width of a skein, but obviously this was not always possible. To make the job more convenient, most early homes had a yarn winder of some sort. Yarn winders generally fall into four categories:

1. Four folding lattice arms, attached to an upright bar which can be unfolded to fit the skein. This type can either be on a table clamp or have a floor stand.
2. An adjustable, revolving, box-shaped top on a floor stand.
3. Two adjustable knobs on an upright bar on a floor stand. The skein fits over the two knobs.
4. Two separate clamps with revolving heads that can be screwed onto a table at a distance to match the skein.

Yarn winder. Cherry with evidence of original red paint, all intact and working order, circa early eighteenth century, $125.00.

To avoid confusion, remember that many terms have been used for yarn winders, such as swift, clockjack, clock reel, reel winder and click reel.

Yarn winders are listed alphabetically by type.

CURRENT
PRICE

DARREL

☐ Circa 1843 .... 285.00

DOUBLE REEL

☐ Mixed woods, on floor stand 200.00
☐ Oak, on floor stand, mortised joints, one adjustable reel 95.00

	CURRENT PRICE
☐ Two wooden reels and table clamp	100.00

DRUM TOP

☐ With hand clock counter mounted on top, on floor stand with black base, turned standard, Shaker	150.00

FOUR SPOKE

☐ Maple	95.00
☐ Mixed woods, primitive, reel in frame, counter, snap mechanism, 27″ × 41″ high	125.00
☐ Mixed woods, hard and soft woods, Shaker, square rail construction, side counter needle, 26″ reel	425.00
☐ Mixed woods, square nail construction, 26″ wheel, Shaker	375.00
☐ Mixed woods, marked	195.00
☐ Mixed woods, primitive, reel in frame, shoe feet, 28″ high	90.00
☐ Mixed woods, primitive, worn counter, 22½″ wheel	85.00
☐ Mixed woods, table clamp, geared counter, turned standard, one fold-back spoke, original red paint	80.00
☐ Oak, poplar and hickory, side counter mechanism	150.00
☐ Painted gray-blue, Windsor turned spokes and standard, original paint	170.00
☐ Pine, on floor stand, primitive	185.00

SIX SPOKE

☐ Oak and ash, clock wheel, carved standard, circa 1860, 38″ high	150.00
☐ Oak and maple, turned spokes, circa 1860, 37″ high	145.00

	CURRENT PRICE
☐ Oak, poplar and hickory, turned spokes, counting wheel, reel, 17″ high	150.00
☐ Red paint, turned standard, counter wheel, original paint, 47″ high	140.00
☐ Walnut, late nineteenth century, 37″ high	165.00
☐ Walnut, cherry and oak, counter mechanism, beaded and carved base, 32″ high	170.00
☐ Walnut, geared counter with paper dial, carved detail on base, 1845, 41¾″ high	185.00

NIDDY NODDY (A simple holder in the shape of an "I")

☐ Hickory, turned, mortised and pinned joints, 18″	85.00
☐ Maple, hand-pegged	65.00
☐ Maple, mortised, 17¼″	75.00

UMBRELLA

☐ Scrimshaw, circa 1830–1870s, with clamp	800.00–1000.00
☐ Walnut with pine standard	155.00

Museums

❀❀❀❀❀❀❀❀❀❀

The following is a partial list of museums in the United States and Canada displaying textiles, needlework and sewing tools.

ARIZONA

Arizona Historical Society, Tucson

CALIFORNIA

Craft and Folk Art Museum, Los Angeles
Lace Museum, Mountain View
Los Angeles Country Museum of Art, Los Angeles
Museum of Vintage Fashion, Lafayette

COLORADO

Denver Art Museum, Denver

CONNECTICUT

Connecticut Historical Society, Hartford
Danbury Scott-Fanton Museum and Historical Society, Inc., Danbury
Mark Twain Memorial; Wadsworth Atheneum, Hartford
Stamford Historical Society, Inc., Stamford

DELAWARE

Henry Francis duPont Winterthur Museum, Winterthur

ILLINOIS

Art Institute of Chicago, Chicago
Wilmette Historical House, Wilmette

INDIANA

Elizabeth Sage Historic Costume Collection, Bloomington
Spring Mill State Park, Mitchell

IOWA

State Historical Society of Iowa, Iowa City

KANSAS

University of Kansas Museum of Art, Lawrence

MAINE

Old Gaol Museum, York

MARYLAND

Baltimore Museum of Art, Baltimore

MASSACHUSETTS

Bostonian Society, Old State House; Museum of Fine Arts, Boston
Essex Institute; Peabody Museum of Salem, Salem

Historic Deerfield, Fabric Hall, Deerfield
Historical Association and Museum, Wenham
Museum of American Textile History, North Andover
Museum of Fine Arts, Boston
Society for the Preservation of New England Antiquities, Boston
Sturbridge Village, Sturbridge
Wenham Historical Association and Museum, Wenham

MICHIGAN

Henry Ford Museum, Dearborn

MINNESOTA

Gibbs Farm Museum, St. Paul
Institute of Arts, Minneapolis

MISSOURI

Laura Ingalls Wilder Home Museum, Mansfield
St. Louis Art Museum, St. Louis

MONTANA

Museum of the Plains Indian, Browning

NEW HAMPSHIRE

New Hampshire Historical Society, Concord

NEW JERSEY

Burlington County Historical Society, Burlington
Newark Museum, Newark

NEW MEXICO

Museum of New Mexico, International Folk Art Foundation Collection, Santa Fe

NEW YORK

Alling Coverlet Museum, Palmyra
Brooklyn Museum, New York
Carnegie Museum, New York
Cooper Union Museum for the Art of Decoration, New York
Cooper-Hewitt Museum. Smithsonian Institution's National Museum of Design, New York
Cooperstown Museum, Cooperstown
Farmers' Museum, Cooperstown
Fenimore House, Cooperstown
Metropolitan Museum of Art, New York
Museum of Modern Art, New York
Museum of Primitive Art, New York
Rochester Memorial Art Gallery, Rochester
Rochester Museum of Arts and Sciences, Rochester
Scalamandre Museum of Textiles, New York
Seneca Falls Historical Society, Seneca Falls
Sleepy Holly Restorations, Tarrytown
Strong Museum, Rochester
Ukrainian Museum, New York
Yeshiva University Museum, New York

NORTH CAROLINA

Biltmore Homespun Shops, Asheville
Gaston County Museum of Art and History, Dallas

OHIO

Allen Art Museum, Oberlin College, Oberlin
Cincinnati Art Museum, Cincinnati
Cleveland Museum of Art, Cleveland
Warren County Historical Society Museum, Lebanon

PENNSYLVANIA

Chester County Historical Society, West Chester
Goldie Paley Design Center, Philadelphia
Moravian Museum of Bethlehem, Bethlehem

Museum of Art, University Museum of Pennsylvania,
   Philadelphia
Pennsylvania Farm Museum of Landis Valley, Lebanon
Philadelphia Museum of Art, Philadelphia

RHODE ISLAND

Slater Mill Historic Site, Pawtucket

TEXAS

Mexican American Cultural Heritage Center, Dallas
Museum of Fine Arts, Houston
Witte Museum, San Antonio

UTAH

Museum of Peoples and Cultures, Provo

VERMONT

Shelbourne Museum, Shelbourne

VIRGINIA

Abby Aldrich Rockefeller Folk Art Collection, Colonial
   Williamsburg, Williamsburg
Harrisonburg-Rockingham Historical Society, Harrison-
   burg
Mary Washington House, Fredericksburg
Mount Vernon Ladies' Association, Mount Vernon
National Tobacco-Textile Museum, Danville
Reuel B. Pritchett Museum, Bridgewater
Valentine Museum, Richmond

WASHINGTON

Henry Art Gallery, Seattle

WASHINGTON, D.C.

Daughters of the American Revolution Museum
Index of American Design
National Gallery of Art
Smithsonian Institution, Museum of American History
Textile Museum

WISCONSIN

Cochrane-Nelson House, Westfield
Helen Allen Textile Collection, Madison
Swarthout Memorial Museum, LaCrosse

CANADA

McCord Museum, Montreal, Quebec
National Museum of Canada, Ottawa, Quebec
Royal Ontario Museum, Toronto, Ontario
Museum of Ethnography, University of British Columbia,
   Vancouver, British Columbia
Hudson's Bay Company Museum, Winnipeg, Manitoba

Bibliography

꙰꙰꙰꙰꙰꙰꙰꙰꙰꙰

Although very few books have been specifically written or published on the tools used in sewing and needlework, the collector can learn more about them by pursuing the vast amount of literature available on sewing and needlework, its place in history, its techniques, its development through the ages and its finished products.

BUTTONS

Albert, Lillian Smith. *A Button Collector's Second Journal*, Yardley, PA: The Cook Printers, 1941.

Albert, Lillian Smith. *The Complete Button Book*, Garden City, NY: Doubleday, 1949.

Brown, Dorothy Foster. *Button Parade*, Chicago, IL: Lightner Publishing Co., 1942.

Ertell, Viviane. *The Colorful World of Buttons*, privately printed.

Ford, Grace Herney. *The Button Collector's History*, Springfield, MA: Pond-Ekberg Company, 1943.

Hughes, Elizabeth and Marion Lester. *The Big Book of Buttons*, privately printed, 1983.

Morgan, W.B. *Calico Button Check List*, 1940.

Nicholls, Florance and Ellis Zacharie. *The Button Hand Book*, Ithaca, NY: Cayuga Press, 1943.

Nicholls, Florance and Ellis Zacharie. *Supplement II and Index to Nichols Button Books*, Ithaca, NY: Art Craft of Ithaca, Inc., 1945.

IRONS

Berney, Esther S. *A Collector's Guide to Pressing Irons and Trivets*, New York: Crown Publishers, Inc., 1977.

Glissman, A.H. *The Evolution of the Sad Iron*, privately printed, 1970.

Jewell, Brian. *Smoothing Irons, A History and Collector's Guide*, Des Moines, IA: Wallace-Homestead, 1977.

FURNITURE—SEWING

Butler, Joseph T. *Field Guide to American Furniture*, New York: Facts on File Publications, 1985.

Comstock, Helen. *American Furniture: Seventeenth, Eighteenth, and Nineteenth Century Styles*, New York: Viking Press, 1962.

Downs, Joseph. *American Furniture: Queen Anne and Chippendale Periods in the Henry Francis du Pont Winterthur Museum*, New York: Macmillan, 1952.

Ketchum, William C. *Desks & Other Pieces*, New York: Alfred A. Knopf, 1982.

Montgomery, Charles F. *American Furniture: The Federal Period in the Henry Francis du Pont Winterthur Museum*, New York: Viking Press, 1966.

Naeve, Milo M. *Identifying American Furniture: A Pictorial Guide to Styles and Terms, Colonial to Contemporary*, American Association for State and Local History, 1981.

Nutting, Wallace. *Furniture Treasure*, 3 Vols., New York: Macmillan, 1928, 1933. Available in reprint.

Rose, Milton C. and Emily Mason. *A Shaker Reader*, New York: Main Street Press/University Press.

Swedberg, Robert W. and Harriett Swedberg. *Country Furniture and Accessories with Prices*, Vols. I and II, Des Moines, IA: Wallace-Homestead, 1983, 1984.

Swedberg, Robert W. and Harriett Swedberg. *American Oak Furniture, Style and Prices*, Vol. II, Des Moines, IA: Wallace-Homestead, 1984.

Swedberg, Robert W. and Harriett Swedberg. *Victorian Furniture*, Vols. I, II, and III, Des Moines, IA: Wallace-Homestead, 1976, 1983, 1985.

Vein, Lyndon C. *Antique Ethnic Furniture*, Des Moines, IA: Wallace-Homestead, 1983.

Zweck, Dia von. *The Woman's Day Dictionary of Furniture*, New York: Citadel Press, 1983.

THIMBLES

Betensley, Bertha. *52 Thimble Patents*, privately printed, 1980.

Dreesman, Cecile. *A Thimble Full*, Netherlands: Cambium, 1983.

Greif, Helmut. *Talks About Thimbles*, Germany: Fingerhutmuseum Creglingen, 1983. (English edition available from Dine-American, Wilmington, DE.)

Holmes, Edwin, F. *A History of Thimbles*, England: Cornwall Books, 1985.

Holmes, Edwin F. *Thimbles*, New York: Till and Macmillan, 1976.

Johnson, Eleanor. *Thimbles*, England: Shires Publications, 1982.

Lundquist, Myrtle A. *The Book of a Thousand Thimbles*, Des Moines, IA: Wallace-Homestead, 1970.

Lundquist, Myrtle A. *Thimble America*, Des Moines, IA: Wallace-Homestead, 1981.

Lundquist, Myrtle A. *Thimble Treasury*, Des Moines, IA: Wallace-Homestead, 1975.

von Heille. John. *Thimble Collector's Encyclopedia*, Wilmington, DE: Din-America, 1983.

GENERAL

Ambuter, Carolyn, *Complete Book of Needlepoint*, New York: Thomas Y. Crowell and Workman Publishing, 1972.

Baker, M.L. *A Handbook of American Crewel Embroidery*, Rutland, VT: Charles E. Tuttle, 1966.

Baker, M.L. *The ABCs of Canvas Embroidery*, Sturbridge, MA: Old Sturbridge Inc., 1968.

Baker, M.L. *The XYZs of Canvas Embroidery*, 2nd ed., Meriden: Meriden Gravure Co., 1971.

Bird, J. & Billinger, L. *Paracas Fabrics and Nazca Needlework, 3rd Century B.C.–3rd Century A.D.*, Washington, D.C.: National Publishing Co., 1954.

Blum, S. (ed.). *Victorian Fashions and Costumes from Harper's Bazaar, 1867–1898*, New York: Dover Publications, 1974.

Carlisle, L.B. *Pieced Work and Applique Quilts of Shelburne Museum*, Shelburne, VT: Shelburne Museum, 1957.

Catlin, G. *Letters and Notes on the Manners, Customs and Conditions of the North American Indians*, London: 1841

Caulfield, S.F.A. *Encyclopedia of Victorian Needlework*, 1887. Reprint, New York: Dover Publications, 1972.

Clabburn, Pamela. *The Needlework Dictionary*, New York: Morrow, 1976.

Cooper, G.R. *The Invention of the Sewing Machine*, Washington, D.C.: Smithsonian Institution Press, 1968.

Davis, M.J. *The Art of Crewel Embroidery*, New York: Crown Publishers, Inc., 1962.

Davis, M.K. and Helen Giammattei. *Needlepoint from America's Great Quilt Designs*, New York: Workman Publishing, 1974.

Fennelly, C. *Textiles in New England, 1790–1840*, Sturbridge, MA: Old Sturbridge Village, 1961.

Finley, R.E. *Old Patchwork Quilts and the Women Who Made Them*, New York: Grosset & Dunlap, 1929 (reprint, Chas. T. Branford Co., Newton Center, MA, 1970).

Garrett, E.D. "American Samplers and Needlework Pictures in the D.A.R. Museum 1739–1806." *Antiques*. 55: 2.

Groves, S. "The History of Needlework Tools," *Country Life*, Hamlyn Publishing Group, 1966.

Harbeson, G.B. *American Needlework*, Coward-McCann, 1938.

Holstein, Jonathan. *The Pieced Quilt—An American Design Tradition*, New York: Dover Publications, 1959.

Hornor, M.M. *The Story of Samplers*, Philadelphia, PA: Philadelphia Museum of Art, 1971.

Hornung, C.P. *Treasury of American Design*, New York: Abrams, 1972. (Two volumes.)

Houck C. and Myron Miller. *American Quilts and How to Make Them*, New York: Scribner, 1975.

Jessup, A.L. *The Sewing Book*, New York: Butterick Publishing, 1913.

Katzenbery, D.S. *The Great American Cover-Up: Counterpanes of the Eighteenth and Nineteenth Centuries*, Baltimore, MD: The Baltimore Museum of Art, 1971.

Kendrick, A.F. *English Needlework*, London: A. & C., Black, 1933.

Lane, R. W. *Woman's Day Book of American Needlework*, New York: Simon and Schuster, 1963.

Leonard, J.N. *Ancient America*, Alexandria, VA: Time-Life Books, 1967.

Lewis, A.A. *The Mountain Artisan Quilting Book*, New York: Macmillan, 1973.

Marion, J.F. *Bicentennial City: Walking Tours of Philadelphia*, Princeton, NJ: Pyne Press, 1974.

Mathews, S.I. *Needlemade Rugs*, New York: Hearthside Press Inc., 1960.

McCall's Needlework in Colour, 4th ed. London: Hamlyn, 1972.

Moore, D.L. *Fashion Through Fashion Plates 1771–1970*, New York: International Publishing Service, 1972.

Morris, B. *Victorian Embroidery*, New York: Thomas Nelson and Sons, 1962.

Naylor, G. *Arts and Crafts Movement*, Cambridge, MA: 1971. Massachusetts Institute of Technology Press, 1971.

Needlecraft—Artistic and Practical, New York: Butterick Publishing, 1890.

Nichols, M. *Encyclopaedia of Embroidery Stitches, Including Crewel*, New York: Dover Publications, 1973.

Peto, F. *American Quilts and Coverlets*, London: Max Parrish & Co., 1949.

Picken, M.B. *The Language of Fashion*, New York: Funk & Wagnalls, 1939.

Risley, C. *Machine Embroidery*, London: Studio Vista, 1961.

Rollins, J.G. *The Early Victorian Needlemakers 1830–1860*, Early Victorian Costume Society, 1969.

Safford, C.L. and Bishop, R. *America's Quilts and Coverlets*, New York: Dutton, 1972.

Schiffer, M.B. *Historical Needlework of Pennsylvania*, New York: Scribner, 1968.

Schuette, M. and Muller Christensen, S. *The Art of Embroidery*, London: Thames & Hudson, 1964.

Seligman, G.S. and Hughes, T. "Domestic Needlework—Its Origins and Customs Throughout the Centuries." *Country Life*, Hamlyn Publishing Group, 1928.

Snook, B. *English Historical Embroidery*, Batsford, London: Mills & Boon, 1960.

Speltz, A. *The Styles of Ornamentation*, New York: Dover Publications, 1959.

Strutt, J. *The Dress and Habits of the People of England*, London: Tabard Press, 1970.

Symonds, M. and L. Preece *Needlework Through the Ages*, London: Hodder & Stoughton, 1928.

Thomas, M. *Mary Thomas's Dictionary of Embroidery*, London: Hodder & Stoughton, 1936.

Wardle, P. *Victorian Lace*, New York: Praeger, 1969.

Whiting, G. *Old-time Tools and Toys of Needlework*, New York: Dover Publications, 1971.

Wilson, E. *Erica Wilson's Embroidery Book*, New York: Scribner, 1973.

Wingate, Dr. I.B. (ed). *Fairchild's Dictionary of Textiles*, New York: Fairchild, 1967.

Index

🪡🪡🪡🪡🪡🪡🪡🪡🪡🪡🪡

The HOUSE OF COLLECTIBLES Series

☐ Please send me the following price guides—
☐ I would like the most current edition of the books listed below.

THE OFFICIAL PRICE GUIDES TO:

☐ 753-3	**American Folk Art** (ID) 1st Ed.	$14.95
☐ 199-3	**American Silver & Silver Plate** 5th Ed.	11.95
☐ 513-1	**Antique Clocks** 3rd Ed.	10.95
☐ 283-3	**Antique & Modern Dolls** 3rd Ed.	10.95
☐ 287-6	**Antique & Modern Firearms** 6th Ed.	11.95
☐ 755-X	**Antiques & Collectibles** 9th Ed.	11.95
☐ 289-2	**Antique Jewelry** 5th Ed.	11.95
☐ 362-7	**Art Deco** (ID) 1st Ed.	14.95
☐ 447-X	**Arts and Crafts: American Decorative Arts, 1894–1923** (ID) 1st Ed.	12.95
☐ 539-5	**Beer Cans & Collectibles** 4th Ed.	7.95
☐ 521-2	**Bottles Old & New** 10th Ed.	10.95
☐ 532-8	**Carnival Glass** 2nd Ed.	10.95
☐ 295-7	**Collectible Cameras** 2nd Ed.	10.95
☐ 548-4	**Collectibles of the '50s & '60s** 1st Ed.	9.95
☐ 740-1	**Collectible Toys** 4th Ed.	10.95
☐ 531-X	**Collector Cars** 7th Ed.	12.95
☐ 538-7	**Collector Handguns** 4th Ed.	14.95
☐ 748-7	**Collector Knives** 9th Ed.	12.95
☐ 361-9	**Collector Plates** 5th Ed.	11.95
☐ 296-5	**Collector Prints** 7th Ed.	12.95
☐ 001-6	**Depression Glass** 2nd Ed.	9.95
☐ 589-1	**Fine Art** 1st Ed.	19.95
☐ 311-2	**Glassware** 3rd Ed.	10.95
☐ 243-4	**Hummel Figurines & Plates** 6th Ed.	10.95
☐ 523-9	**Kitchen Collectibles** 2nd Ed.	10.95
☐ 080-6	**Memorabilia of Elvis Presley and The Beatles** 1st Ed.	10.95
☐ 291-4	**Military Collectibles** 5th Ed.	11.95
☐ 525-5	**Music Collectibles** 6th Ed.	11.95
☐ 313-9	**Old Books & Autographs** 7th Ed.	11.95
☐ 298-1	**Oriental Collectibles** 3rd Ed.	11.95
☐ 761-4	**Overstreet Comic Book** 18th Ed.	12.95
☐ 522-0	**Paperbacks & Magazines** 1st Ed.	10.95
☐ 297-3	**Paper Collectibles** 5th Ed.	10.95
☐ 744-6	**Political Memorabilia** 1st Ed.	10.95
☐ 529-8	**Pottery & Porcelain** 6th Ed.	11.95
☐ 524-7	**Radio, TV & Movie Memorabilia** 3rd Ed.	11.95
☐ 081-4	**Records** 8th Ed.	16.95
☐ 763-0	**Royal Doulton** 6th Ed.	12.95
☐ 280-9	**Science Fiction & Fantasy Collectibles** 2nd Ed.	10.95
☐ 747-9	**Sewing Collectibles** 1st Ed.	8.95
☐ 358-9	**Star Trek/Star Wars Collectibles** 2nd Ed.	8.95
☐ 086-5	**Watches** 8th Ed.	12.95
☐ 248-5	**Wicker** 3rd Ed.	10.95

THE OFFICIAL:

☐ 760-6	**Directory to U.S. Flea Markets** 2nd Ed.	5.95
☐ 365-1	**Encyclopedia of Antiques** 1st Ed.	9.95
☐ 369-4	**Guide to Buying and Selling Antiques** 1st Ed.	9.95
☐ 414-3	**Identification Guide to Early American Furniture** 1st Ed.	9.95
☐ 413-5	**Identification Guide to Glassware** 1st Ed.	9.95
☐ 412-7	**Identification Guide to Pottery & Porcelain** 1st Ed.	$9.95
☐ 415-1	**Identification Guide to Victorian Furniture** 1st Ed.	9.95

THE OFFICIAL (SMALL SIZE) PRICE GUIDES TO:

☐ 309-0	**Antiques & Flea Markets** 4th Ed.	4.95
☐ 269-8	**Antique Jewelry** 3rd Ed.	4.95
☐ 085-7	**Baseball Cards** 8th Ed.	4.95
☐ 647-2	**Bottles** 3rd Ed.	4.95
☐ 544-1	**Cars & Trucks** 3rd Ed.	5.95
☐ 519-0	**Collectible Americana** 2nd Ed.	4.95
☐ 294-9	**Collectible Records** 3rd Ed.	4.95
☐ 306-6	**Dolls** 4th Ed.	4.95
☐ 762-2	**Football Cards** 8th Ed.	4.95
☐ 540-9	**Glassware** 3rd Ed.	4.95
☐ 526-3	**Hummels** 4th Ed.	4.95
☐ 279-5	**Military Collectibles** 3rd Ed.	4.95
☐ 764-9	**Overstreet Comic Book Companion** 2nd Ed.	4.95
☐ 278-7	**Pocket Knives** 3rd Ed.	4.95
☐ 527-1	**Scouting Collectibles** 4th Ed.	4.95
☐ 494-1	**Star Trek/Star Wars Collectibles** 3rd Ed.	3.95
☐ 088-1	**Toys** 5th Ed.	4.95

THE OFFICIAL BLACKBOOK PRICE GUIDES OF:

☐ 092-X	**U.S. Coins** 27th Ed.	4.95
☐ 095-4	**U.S. Paper Money** 21st Ed.	4.95
☐ 098-9	**U.S. Postage Stamps** 11th Ed.	4.95

THE OFFICIAL INVESTORS GUIDE TO BUYING & SELLING:

☐ 534-4	**Gold, Silver & Diamonds** 2nd Ed.	12.95
☐ 535-2	**Gold Coins** 2nd Ed.	12.95
☐ 536-0	**Silver Coins** 2nd Ed.	12.95
☐ 537-9	**Silver Dollars** 2nd Ed.	12.95

THE OFFICIAL NUMISMATIC GUIDE SERIES:

☐ 254-X	**The Official Guide to Detecting Counterfeit Money** 2nd Ed.	7.95
☐ 257-4	**The Official Guide to Mint Errors** 4th Ed.	7.95

SPECIAL INTEREST SERIES:

☐ 506-9	**From Hearth to Cookstove** 3rd Ed.	17.95
☐ 504-2	**On Method Acting** 8th Printing	6.95

TOTAL	

SEE REVERSE SIDE FOR ORDERING INSTRUCTIONS